WRITING FOR RESILIENCE

Finding the Courage to Bounce Back

Charmaine Pollard

Consulting Editor: Diana McMahon Collis in association with 'Jericho Writers'.

This book includes fictional case studies for illustrative purposes, which are the product of the author's imagination. Any resemblance to actual persons, living or dead, or actual events is purely coincidental.

In instances where the writing and experiences of real-life workshop participants have been used, some names have been changed according to the wishes of those individuals.

This publication is meant as a source of valuable information for the reader, however it is not meant as a substitute for direct expert assistance. If such level of assistance is required, the services of a competent professional should be sought.

Illustrations by Simon Goodway

ISBN: 9798580106915

First edition.

Printed by Charmaine Pollard Counselling in Great Britain

For My Husband, Miss Vera, Nat, Aunt Nav and Beautiful.

In memory of Lynda Field, a beautiful soul and an inspirational life coach.

Foreword

I am delighted to endorse this book by Charmaine Pollard.

For many years, Charmaine has shared her skills, knowledge and personal qualities with groups and individuals from all backgrounds and walks of life. Under her guidance, people are empowered to find the confidence and resilience to lead more fulfilling lives. This book will enable many more of us to experience the power of the techniques she has developed.

Charmaine was already a highly experienced therapist when she discovered the potential of writing as an additional therapeutic tool. As she says, she was amazed at how quickly and easily she could pour herself out onto the page. Expressive writing can give us quick and direct access to our subconscious mind. It can be challenging and exciting. And when something is both challenging and exciting, we need guidance to explore it safely. That is what Charmaine offers here.

Her book is entitled Writing for Resilience: Finding the Courage to Bounce Back. 'Courage' comes from the French word 'coeur', meaning 'heart', and expressive writing comes, as Charmaine's work does, directly from the heart. This is where we will find the courage to be our best – and most authentic – selves.

The terrain of therapeutic writing is a large one. In this book, Charmaine acts as the perfect guide, sharing the path she has found through the many practices on offer. As we travel with her, she invites us to ask ourselves questions in a way that will yield new answers. She introduces writing by people who have attended her groups, and explains how our writing can speak back to us. Every chapter takes the reader step-by-step on a journey of self-discovery.

Anyone who works carefully through the writing exercises she suggests will come away with insights, inspiration and confidence to make informed changes. Charmaine has tried and tested all the techniques she shares here, and she and her clients are testimony to their power to build resilience.

Don't hesitate: pick up your pen, find some paper and begin! You are in good hands.

Victoria Field
Writer and Poetry Therapist

Acknowledgments

Thank you to:

My family: you have taught me so many valuable life lessons. I love you.

My friends: you have been – and will always be – the most amazing part of my journey.

My former mentor supervisor, Victoria Field: your encouragement and inspiration are such precious gifts. You are a phenomenal woman!

My copyeditor, Kate McBarron: your enthusiasm, insight and skill on this project has been invaluable. It is such a pleasure to work with you.

Brother Steve: your sense of humour puts that huge smile on my face. RIP.

Daneshia Lowther: your inspiration for key exercises has been incredible. I am grateful for your input.

Ms Susan Edwards (Vice Principal): for your willingness to take a risk and offer the pupils at Richmond Park Academy a creative way to express their emotions, tackle difficult issues and increase their confidence.

My colleagues, the RiseUp CIC team: doing amazing work in prisons to promote self-esteem and increase positive behaviour and employability skills.

Poets: for giving permission for your words to be included in this book. It truly is an honour and privilege. Thank you to Victoria Field, Portia Nelson, Linda Pastan, Vicki Feaver, Bethany Rivers, Natasha Lynne Vogdes, J. Ruth Gendler, Imelda Maguire, Roger Robinson and the Estate of Langston Hughes.

Contributors: a massive thank you to all of you who have contributed to this book; it would not exist without you. Each chapter has managed to capture some of the energy and vigour from our sessions. Those precious moments have been transformative, and reading over your pieces and poems has brought back fond memories of our time together. Keep on writing. Honour that courageous and resilient part of you, which is now being woven, beautifully, into the lives of others.

Contents

Introduction

Welcome to *Writing for Resilience: Finding the Courage to Bounce Back*. This workbook is for anyone who yearns to be more resilient and would like to learn about themselves through writing. It features simple, yet thought-provoking writing activities, poetry and self-assessments that have been chosen to inspire insights and growth.

With only a pen and a piece of paper, you can discover so much about yourself and the world around you. This book will take you on a journey of self-discovery. You will realise, through your own writing, that you already have a high level of courage and resilience. You have survived so much! As you continue to explore and strengthen your resilience, through time and effort, you will be able to create your own unique survival guide to help overcome future obstacles.

Writing as therapy

The decision to write this book occurred during the life of a poetry therapy group for women survivors of trauma, in central London. Together, we decided that we wanted to offer hope to those who had been through challenging circumstances, as well as introduce other people to this fantastic resource: writing-as-therapy.

As a poetry therapist, myself, I have facilitated numerous poetry therapy workshops, in a wide variety of contexts. I have worked with survivors of domestic and sexual violence; people who misuse substances; prisoners; dementia sufferers and their carers; people living with mental illness; students at secondary schools and in further education; orthodox Jews and individuals with a general interest in writing and wellbeing.

Through my work, I have recognised that we all struggle with many of the same issues, irrespective of race, class, sexual orientation, education, gender or culture. The conversations and discussions I have experienced – particularly relating to resilience and how people summon the courage to bounce back from their difficulties – have been captivating, encouraging and heartfelt. I have seen, as well, that writing can play a powerful role in our journeys of self-discovery.

Writing for therapy is not like other types of writing. In simple terms, it is about using the written word to promote healing and growth. By writing and reflecting on our own words, we can gain a deeper understanding of ourselves and, in turn, prepare for change.

I was first introduced to writing as therapy more than ten years ago, when I attended a one-day conference for the arts. It amazed me how quickly and easily I could pour myself out, onto the page. The process of writing seemed to bring alive feelings and thoughts I had not even considered. It gave me immediate insights. Reflecting on my words afterwards then helped me to delve even deeper.

As a counsellor, I saw immediately that writing was a valuable tool for healing and personal development; a tool that could get quickly to the heart of things, in a way that I had not encountered before. I was eager to learn more and – years later – qualified as a certified poetry therapist with the USA-based International Federation for Biblio/Poetry Therapy (IFBPT).

Nowadays, when I attend workshops for my own personal development – in addition to learning new skills – I embrace their practical, easy-to-follow approach, which helps me consider different perspectives. My hope in writing this book is that you will benefit from a similar experience. Within these pages there are many opportunities for your own writing and reflection. I trust you will also find inspiration from reading pieces of writing by other men and women, whom I have been privileged to meet through my work. I am grateful that they have kindly agreed to share their stories. Their words can inspire hope and help to remind us of the strength of the human spirit.

How to use this book

You may be new to writing, a seasoned writer, or returning from a writing break. Whichever category you are in, I urge you to read the first chapter of this book carefully. It will help you to write safely and understand the value of using words in a therapeutic way.

Glossary

You will find a **glossary** at the end of the book, which explains various terms that may be unfamiliar to you. Words or phrases included in the glossary have an asterisk (*) next to them, in the main text of the book.

It is worth noting that 'writing as therapy' has many different names, which can cause confusion. Practitioners call their craft different things, depending on context and the type of writing involved. You may hear phrases like: 'writing for wellbeing', 'poetry therapy', 'journal therapy', 'therapeutic writing' and 'expressive writing'. While there are subtle differences between these, they are all intended to reflect the interactive use of writing – and literature – to promote growth and healing.

You may have read other self-help books, or this may be your first. As in life, not everything that you read about will work for you, and that is fine. Take what you need from this book. I suggest you move at your own pace and pause at regular intervals, as you work your way through the activities.

To encourage you to take a break, you will see these words:

B r e a t h i n g   S p a c e.

Feel free to carry out the given instructions, at those points, or even take a longer break if necessary, returning to the writing when you feel able. Consider revisiting a chapter, perhaps, to see if your perspective has changed. You will develop your own flow. Your writing will tell you where to go.

Some writing exercises may be time-limited. If a time limit has not been given, write until you have exhausted your ideas, or come to a natural pause. Try to avoid one-word answers, unless directed to give those.

You may find some of the exercises challenging, or experience resistance towards a writing prompt*. Your instinct might tell you to ignore the prompt and write something else. Follow your instincts – the writing prompts are there simply to get you started. But do pay attention to any resistance, and feel free to write about it or revisit the prompt later. I have gained a significant amount of insight from revisiting writing prompts that I initially resisted!

Put yourself first

Self-help has to start with you, but it can begin easily enough. You simply have to believe that you are the most important person in your life. Equally, the most important relationship you have, is the one you have with yourself.

Once these beliefs are in place, true transformation can occur.

People are sometimes absolutely ready for such a transformation; at other times change can seem scary. Only you will know which stage you are at. I can assure you, though, that if you follow the instructions in this book – whenever you are ready – and stay with the process, this will all enhance the way you feel and help with any changes you hope to make.

You may like to spend some time reflecting, now – through your own writing – on your main motivation for reading this book.

Do you want to be more assertive?
Do you wish you could ask for what you want in your relationships?
Do you simply wish to be better at problem-solving?

There may be a range of reasons. Whatever your motivation, take a moment to write it down now, just for you. My advice is: be specific!

- What has been my motivation for reading this book?

- What do I hope to achieve by reading this book?

Well done for putting yourself first and setting aside the time to read this book. I sincerely hope that you enjoy your journey of self-discovery. We will work, in Chapter 1, on taking a closer look at how writing can help with self-development, as well as ways you can take care of yourself while writing.

* Please refer to the glossary for definitions of asterisked terms.

Chapter 1

Understanding the value of writing

I can shake off everything as I write, my sorrows disappear,
my courage is reborn.
Anne Frank

Writing is an exceptionally powerful tool. It bears witness to our experiences, which include successes, desires, difficulties and frustrations. When used in a therapeutic way, it can offer significant health and wellbeing benefits. For many years, experts from the 'writing for health and wellbeing' community have been investigating these benefits. Their research has shown that writing can help people in a wide variety of circumstances, from those dealing with terminal illness or the aftermath of violent crime, to students facing first-year transitions.

One such researcher is Dr James Pennebaker – a social psychologist and author of numerous books, including *Opening Up: The Healing Power of Expressing Emotions* and *Writing to Heal*. He also co-authored *Writing it Down*, with Joshua Smyth. Pennebaker is a pioneer in the study of 'expressive writing'. His research has shown that this particular type of writing can help to improve both mental health and physical health. Pennebaker talks about the value of writing down and 'labelling' your feelings. He explains that, by ordering your experiences into a coherent story, you make them easier to process.

Expressive writing is just one form of therapeutic writing. Another is poetry therapy – a highly versatile approach which, in my experience, can be extremely useful for those who wish to increase their confidence and build resilience.

Why poetry?

Poems are excellent vehicles for change. As safe containers for your most powerful and intimate thoughts, feelings and behaviours, they can help you to tell your story. The process of reading and writing poetry offers valuable insights, allowing you to increase your self-awareness and – in turn – build resilience.

Roger Robinson, a British-Caribbean poet, writer and performer, who won the 2019 T.S. Eliot prize with *A Portable Paradise*, says in a manifesto entitled Success is on You, which he wrote for *The Poetry Review* (The Guilford Press, 1990):

'The poet's job is to translate unspeakable things on the page.'

Commenting on this manifesto in an interview, Robinson added:

'Poets can touch hearts and minds; they translate trauma into something people can face.'

For these reasons, poems can be a useful 'way in' to discuss difficulties, issues and concerns.

You will find that many of the poems and pieces of writing featured in this book are written by participants who have attended my poetry therapy groups. They created their own pieces of writing by responding spontaneously to poems that inspired them. Reading poetry, discussing it, and writing in response to it, are fundamental parts of poetry therapy. When we read a poem, something happens within us. We react using our hearts and minds – and sometimes even our bodies. We can use these same feelings, thoughts and sensations to fuel our own writing.

Geri Chavis, in her book *Poetry and Story Therapy: The Healing Power of Creative Expression* (Jessica Kingsley, 2011), explains that writing in response to a poem '…is one of the most effective ways to encourage exploration'. She goes on to say:

'From their writing, participants almost always expand or deepen their emotional, cognitive and visceral responses to meaningful elements of a poem and make the poem, in a sense, their own.'

Reading poetry can bring a significant amount of relief and comfort. Perhaps you can recall a poem that has offered you encouragement during difficult times. You might be someone who is able to recite scripture from a holy book. The Bible, for example, is full of poetry; you may choose to recite one of its many psalms, or a memorable verse. Alternatively, you may be familiar with the lyrics of a song, or rap, that provides solace or inspiration.

- Find a poem, piece of scripture or song that gives you comfort. Write it out in full and then read it aloud.

In her book, *Therapeutic Journal Writing: An Introduction for Professionals* (Jessica Kingsley Publishers, 2011), author Kate Thompson suggests that reading journals 'out loud' is powerful and affirming. Likewise, it can be worthwhile reading aloud a poem you have written. You will likely hear the words in a new way and make connections – or uncover emotions – that you were not aware of whilst writing.

By now, you will be starting to understand the value of therapeutic writing as a personal development tool. I asked participants at one of my workshops to think about the ways in which poetry helps them. Here are some of their responses:

- Expressing emotions and providing opportunities for self-reflection

- Ordering thinking

- Clarifying thoughts and feelings

- Making sense of experiences

- Remembering successes

- Facing up to difficult situations

- Bringing a sense of calm; reducing anxieties

- Enhancing creativity

- Building resilience – it reminds you of how far you have travelled

- Lifting your mood

- Making better decisions

- Venting and expressing difficult emotions; 'screaming' on the page.

As you make your way through this book, my hope is that you will experience many – if not all – of these benefits, for yourself.

You can write

People write for many reasons. For some, writing is a core part of their job or academic studies. For others, writing will extend only as far as the creation of a weekly shopping list, sending text messages to friends, or posting on social media. Writing is present in all of our lives, to a greater or lesser extent. For any reader who feels they cannot write well enough to complete the activities in this book, now is the time to shed that belief!

For the type of writing you will be doing here, there will be no need to worry about grammar, spelling, punctuation or style.

Put aside any negative comments you may have heard at school. Whatever your level of education – so long as you can form thoughts that make sense to you and mark them on the page – you can reap the rewards of this book.

The writing I invite you to do, here, is a personal process; it is for *you* and your development. You may decide, later, that some of your work can be developed, edited or rewritten, so it could be shared more widely. However, the primary focus of this type of writing is for you to write spontaneously and _write from your heart._

Preparing to write

Writing for therapeutic purposes requires little to get started. All you need is a piece of paper and something to write with – preferably something that feels comfortable in your hand. Many of us, nowadays, write using a keyboard or electronic device; we can often type faster than our thoughts can form themselves! Having said that, therapeutic writing is more beneficial when you write by hand. There is a lot to be said for using a pen or pencil and piece of paper. The hand moving over the page feels cathartic, in a way that is hard to achieve using electronic devices.

Natalie Goldberg, author of *Writing Down the Bones: Freeing the Writer Within* (Shambhala Publications, Inc., 1986), suggests that, 'Handwriting is more connected with the movement of the heart'. We may also consider that the way your writing shows up on the page can offer insights into underlying emotions and unconscious processes. From my own experience, I know that, when my writing looks more hurried or is messier than usual, it is a sign that I need to slow down and take time out for myself.

Where you choose to write is also an important consideration, when getting ready for a writing session. Some people write in cafés, libraries or the local park. You may have a particular place in your home, away from flatmates, your children, your partner, or other family members; somewhere that feels comfortable and private. Wherever you choose, it is worth considering the ambience of the setting, for when you write. Are you happy with the lighting? You may want some inspiring music on, in the background, or perhaps prefer to write in silence.

Taking into account the time of day is also important. When are you most energised? Are you a 'morning' or 'evening' person? Julia Cameron, author of *The Artist's Way: A Course in Discovering and Recovering Your Creative Self* (Pan Books, 1995), promotes a practice of writing 'morning pages'. This involves three pages of stream-of-consciousness writing* – written by hand – first thing in the morning, without censoring or editing any words. You might find that writing at the beginning of the day works well for you, particularly if you easily get the opportunity to do so.

Finally, you may decide that you want to write with a writing partner, or in a group, rather than alone. It can be motivating to know that someone else is committed to regular writing sessions with you. You may, however, prefer the idea of having time to yourself while you write. This is a matter of personal choice.

Self-care when writing

I will be inviting you, in this book, to complete various exercises that will challenge both your beliefs and the very core of who you are. These exercises will encourage, exploration, self-expression and creativity. You may find that your emotions are roused and, at times, may well benefit from having a box of tissues handy. This is perfectly natural. Writing inevitably evokes memories and stirs up reactions.

Whilst therapeutic writing is beneficial for working with and processing emotions, you may occasionally feel unable to write about a difficult experience. If you find yourself becoming overwhelmed, pay attention to your feelings and practise self-care. Stop writing – immediately – and carry out a grounding technique, such as paying attention to your surroundings. Notice your feet on the floor and feel the chair supporting your back; describe out loud the room or space you are in. Note the colours you see and the objects around you. Afterwards, you may wish to distract yourself, by having a chat with a friend or family member. You could also refer to the poem, passage of scripture or song that you wrote down earlier in this chapter.

When writing for therapeutic purposes, it is always worth having a self-care activity in place, to enjoy afterwards. Look at the activities that follow and consider which of these you might like to do at the end of your writing session. Should your writing take you to an unexpected place, having a feel-good activity already planned will help to lift your mood.

Self-care activities

Meet a friend: Why not meet up with a friend or relative for coffee, or visit a museum or art gallery together? Alternatively, connect with a friend online, by using apps such as Zoom, Facetime or WhatsApp. Make sure this is someone whose company you enjoy!

Focus on your strengths: You may have a natural tendency to bring yourself down, but, just for today, try to focus on your strengths. Make a long list of them!

Do something creative: Paint a picture; buy a colouring book and start colouring; get your old recorder or keyboard out; sing a song… Whatever you choose, do something creative, and pay attention to how your energy changes.

Listen to soothing music or the sounds of nature: Music has the power to lift your mood. Soft, soothing music can lower your stress levels and help you to relax. Natural sounds can sometimes have a similar effect.

Do something physical: Go for a walk or a run; attend a dance class; go swimming… Exercise releases feel-good hormones and is a great way to rid yourself of so-called 'negative' emotions.

Treat yourself: Do something you have been meaning to do for a long time. This might include treating yourself to a new pair of jeans, or a new book; visiting a sauna or researching and going for a new hairstyle. Allow yourself to enjoy the experience and come out feeling good!

Before beginning writing, if you are unsure about where any of your writing might lead, take some time to complete the sentence stems* that follow, below. Go with your first thoughts and allow whatever comes into your head to flow out onto the page:

- I feel safe when…

- If strong emotions or thoughts arise, during writing exercises, I can…

- The people who can support me are…

- Three things I can do to help myself are…

As you work your way through this book, remember that, if your writing stirs up emotions and you feel overwhelmed, you can carry out one of the self-care activities listed above, immediately - or use another, nurturing activity of your choice. Some people also find it useful to seek professional help, for example speaking to a General Practitioner (GP) or finding a counsellor. This can be particularly helpful if you are struggling to cope with a traumatic experience, or other, challenging situation. Looking after yourself is the priority!

The power of reflective writing

So far, I have talked about the value of poetry as a therapeutic tool, how you can prepare yourself to write, and some self-care essentials. Now, it is worth considering a particular type of writing that I will be inviting you to try throughout this book: reflective writing.

This form of reflection involves reading a piece of writing – which may have been written by you, or someone else – and exploring your own thoughts and feelings towards it. Taking part in this process is a vital step on your journey of self-discovery. Reflecting in this way gives you the chance to examine stories and situations from your life, at a deeper level, resulting in gaining valuable insights. Kathleen Adams, in her book, *Journal Therapy for Calming Anxiety: 366 Prompts to Help Reduce Stress and Create Inner Peace* (Sterling Publishing Company, 2020), comments that 'the reflection write harvests insight. It is the express elevator to clarity'. Meanwhile, Kate Thompson suggests, in her book, *Therapeutic Journal Writing: An Introduction for Professionals* (Jessica Kingsley Publishers, 2011), that your reflective responses can be '…the first stirrings of recognition and healing and of making connections to the self'.

Reflective writing allows you to access emotions you were not aware of previously. It is equivalent to a counsellor hearing you share an experience and then enquiring about your feelings, or helping you make connections to previous life events.

As an example, an individual may find it difficult to maintain a long-term relationship of their own, because they witnessed a toxic relationship between their parents when growing up. On an unconscious level, this person may fear ending up like their parents. However, they may only discover this consciously after reflecting on their family history and their feelings about it.

To be able to move forward from a challenging situation or self-defeating habit, we may need to connect with the emotion, name it, and explore it further, rather than focus purely on the facts or actions that took place. We also need to understand the roots of a particular behaviour. The event itself is only one part of the overall 'story'. How we respond to that event on an emotional level will play a part in guiding our actions in the future.

To journal or not to journal

One place where reflective writing happens naturally is in a journal. This is the final element to consider, before we start on the path to building resilience.

A journal is an excellent container for thoughts, feelings and achievements, alongside the daily events of your life. It is a safe space in which you can offload, take risks and express emotions at any time of the day or night. Avid journal writers often describe their journal as a companion, as their best friend or even as their therapist. Just like a therapist, your journal will embrace what is being shared and challenge some of your beliefs, without judgement or criticism. Kathleen Adams, author of *Journal to the Self: Twenty-Two Paths to Personal Growth* (Warner Books, 1990), refers to her journal as, 'the 79 ¢ therapist', because she can purchase a notebook for less than a dollar.

Many people keep journals or diaries for several years and write in them daily, while others only record key emotions or events. Others add collages, photos and inspiring words, or quotes. There is no right or wrong way to keep a journal!

In her poem, below, Gila suggests challenging yourself to write through the pain.

Take Risks

Take risks
said writing coach
to the sceptic
so she did
push your boundaries
said she
write through the pain
challenge yourself
keep a journal
notice
the bare bones
put fat on it
own your story
and when one notepad is filled
she'll just hand you another

Gila

Keeping a journal or notebook is also a good way to create a habit of writing. If you write on a regular basis you will feel the benefits of therapeutic writing much more quickly; this is true even if you only write for five minutes a day. It is a bit like exercising. If you go to the gym once, then you might feel better for a short time. If you attend on a regular basis, then you can enjoy longer-lasting change.

In my experience, journaling is essential for enhancing self-awareness, self-confidence and – ultimately – resilience.

- Do you keep a journal or a diary? If yes, what are your main reasons for doing so? If no, what is standing in your way? How can you overcome this?

As you go through this book, I highly recommend that you keep a journal of your experiences. It will be a great resource – I promise! You will have a record of your starting point – where you made a decision to change. You will also have the opportunity to record your struggles and how you coped with them. From this, you can identify your sources of resilience and then decide how to use these tools to tackle any future bumps in the road. A journal can be a reminder of how far you have travelled and can motivate you to move on. I suggest you start a new journal or notebook specifically to accompany this book. As you work your way through each chapter, be sure to write down the date.

When keeping a journal, privacy and security are important. If you have journaled before and given up, it may have been because your privacy was compromised. If so, I urge you to consider the precautions you can take, now, to keep your new journal away from prying eyes. It will be worth the effort!

Now that you have finished working through this chapter, review the writing you have done and complete the following sentence stem:

- The main insight I gained from this chapter…

Take a moment, now, to acknowledge all your hard work.

Finally, if you would like a reminder – at any point – about the value of writing, you may wish to refer to Victoria Field's poem below, first featured in **Writing Works:** *A Resource Handbook for Therapeutic Writing Workshops and Activities*, edited by Gillie Bolton, Victoria Field and Kate Thompson (Jessica Kingsley Publishers, 2006).

Why Writing?

It says the unsayable.
Gives voice to the voiceless.
It's a lifetime's work –
Handiwork, whole body work.

It gives form to chaos.
It reflects the present moment,
Changes the past
And creates the future.

It can exist forever
Or completely disappear.
It is what it is.
It can always be changed.

It's where the impossible
Becomes the possible.
It takes us out of ourselves
And into ourselves.

It is where we live our unlived lives,
Where we can surprise ourselves.
It is fire.
Only we can write our writing.

Victoria Field
Reproduced with permission from Victoria Field.

To sum up...

- Writing is powerful, so do practise self-care when necessary.

- Poetry is an excellent catalyst for discussion, writing and self-development.

- Journaling and keeping track of your progress is crucial.

In the next chapter, we will define resilience and begin to look at some of the factors that can help you to bounce back more easily.

* Please refer to the glossary for definitions of asterisked terms.

Chapter 2

Defining resilience

Do not judge me by my successes, judge me by how many times
I fell down and got back up again.
Nelson Mandela

What is resilience?

We live in extremely challenging and uncertain times. As individuals, some of us may struggle with issues such as illness or disability. Others may struggle with poverty, displacement, racism, or homophobia – and versions of discrimination that appear at various levels. Some people may be contending with violence – or the fear of violence in their personal lives. There are also global threats, such as war, terrorism, social unrest, diseases, climate change and economic crises. Fear can enter our homes through many different formats these days – such as on our televisions, computers, smartphones and tablets.

Award-winning American poet and pacifist, William Stafford, offers us one perspective on how we might cope with such challenges, in his poem 'The Way It Is' – featured in his collection *The Way It Is: New and Selected Poems* (Graywolf Press, 2006). Stafford talks about tragedies happening and people getting hurt and getting old, along with suffering and dying. We will all experience some of these issues in our lives; they are parts of life. Stafford nonetheless also refers to the 'thread' we hold on to, throughout our lives. This thread is constant. No matter what happens, 'you don't ever let go of the thread'.

Reflect for a moment on what has helped you during times of tragedy or when you have been hurt. How did you get back up again? What thread did you hold on to?

After difficult times, we so often say, 'I just got on with it' or 'I don't know how I got through it'. It is crucial that you identify what you did, specifically. Name the inner resources you fell back on, the words you said to yourself to help you keep going and the steps you took to recover.

When in the middle of a crisis or difficulty, we can start to believe that other people have everything under control – that they have 'got it all together', while we have not. We can often feel much worse because of this belief. Yet we know that no two people, who are faced with the same set of circumstances, will respond in the same way. Each one of us has a different threshold. Some situations that are manageable to one individual will be distressing to another.

Why do some people bounce back relatively easily from adversity, tragedies and trauma? What helps them to get through such tough circumstances? The answer can be expressed in one word: 'resilience'.

There are many definitions of resilience. I find the *Oxford Dictionaries* definition to be helpful. It describes resilience as, '1 The capacity to recover quickly from difficulties; toughness. 2 The ability of a substance or object to spring back into shape; elasticity'. Meanwhile, in his book *Build Your Resilience* (Hodder Education, 2012), author Donald Robertson cites the researchers Masten, Cutuli, Herbers and Reed, when he defines resilience as, 'Patterns of positive adaptation during or following significant adversity'. In essence, resilience is the ability to bounce back from difficult situations without experiencing long-term, adverse effects.

We all have a capacity for resilience, even though our own resources might often seem scattered and difficult to accept. Throughout this book, we will examine some of your thoughts, feelings and behaviours, and sharpen your tools for survival. Through your own writing, the writing of others and self-reflection, you will learn skills that can enhance your ability to positively adapt and cope with adversity and change.

In a moment, we will go through an exercise that involves writing in response to a poem. First, take a look at Paulette's definition of resilience, in the poem on the next page:

Resilience

The old wood heap had its dangers -
Snakes, spiders, sudden collapse
But we only saw it as adventure.

The hill on the farm was the Matterhorn of our childhood,
We found a long board and the wheels from the old pram,
And hammered our way to a go-cart of promise.

The screaming delight as we flew our way
Through the long grass
And into infinity.

For every ride, the scrapes and scratches
Read their way to wisdom.
We added brakes, we refined the path
Around the old stumps and over the cow tracks.

The dirt you wore was honour.
If it came with tears, help was about
To dust you off and reassure

That, when we are ready to know it,
Every fall can teach us how to make the next ride
Better than the last.
The thrill in taking it, is living.

Paulette Brooks

Writing in response to a poem

Throughout this book, there are various activities in which you will be invited to read a poem and write about your experience of it, afterwards. It is important that you focus on your response to the poem, emotionally or cognitively, rather than critiquing the poem.

Author and poetry therapist, Victoria Field, suggests the following, when writing in response to a poem, 'Read the poem slowly and, if possible, aloud, to feel the words in your mouth and get a sense of its rhythms and cadences. Pay attention to any emotions or memories it stirs in you. Imagine telling someone else about how you react to the poem. What would you say?'

- Re-read 'Resilience' by Paulette Brooks. Allow the images to come to life.

- Take a few minutes and stay with the memories and emotions, then write about your first bike ride, scooter, skateboard or makeshift go-cart. Basically, write about any mode of transport with wheels, where you used your own body and/or judgement to ride, drive or stay on. Write for fifteen minutes.

- What did any falls, stalls or setbacks teach you?

- Complete the following sentence stem:

- I dust myself off so…

- Read over your responses and complete the following sentence stem:

- Now that I have read what I have written, I am aware/feel…

- Describe your understanding of resilience by completing the following sentence stem:

Resilience is…

Now that you have a better understanding of resilience and have defined it in your own words, we are going to use a simple method to check your current resilience levels. Using the Resilience Levels Checker on the next page, you will be able to give yourself a resilience score, which you can use to help measure your progress. We will check resilience levels again, near the end of this book.

Resilience Levels Checker

Look at the resilience scale, which represents the range of emotions and thoughts from your lowest levels of resilience to your highest. Think about where you would generally place yourself on that scale.

Your resilience at its lowest

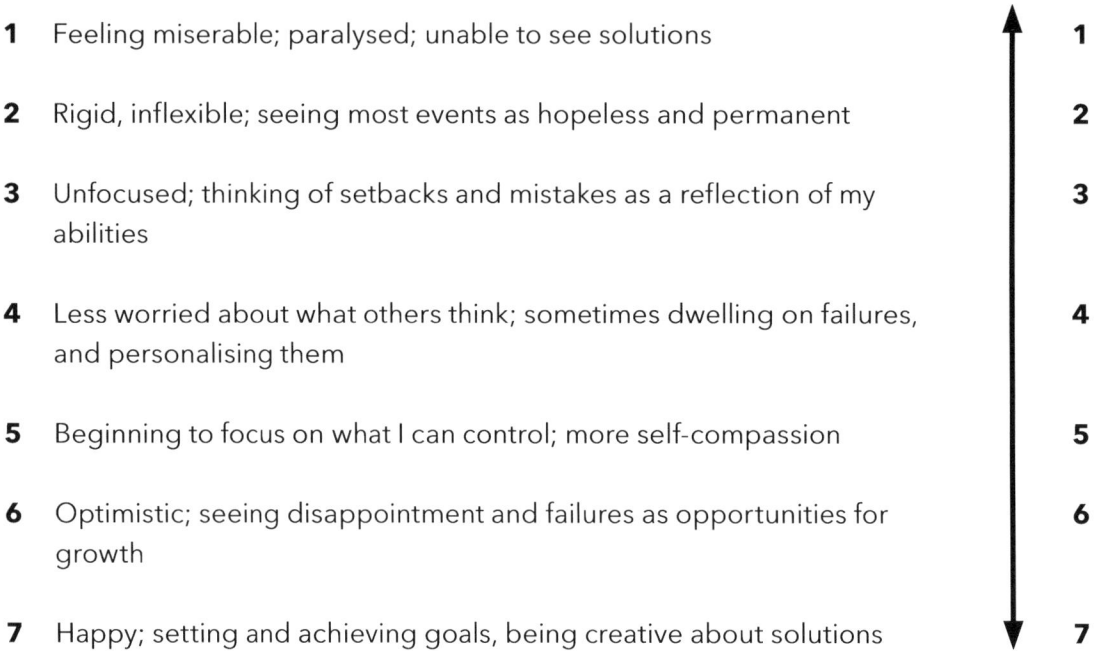

1 Feeling miserable; paralysed; unable to see solutions **1**

2 Rigid, inflexible; seeing most events as hopeless and permanent **2**

3 Unfocused; thinking of setbacks and mistakes as a reflection of my abilities **3**

4 Less worried about what others think; sometimes dwelling on failures, and personalising them **4**

5 Beginning to focus on what I can control; more self-compassion **5**

6 Optimistic; seeing disappointment and failures as opportunities for growth **6**

7 Happy; setting and achieving goals, being creative about solutions **7**

Your resilience at its highest

Did you place yourself at level 1, feeling miserable and paralysed? Or were you at level 5, becoming more self-compassionate and taking back control of how you generally respond to adverse situations? If your score was in the lower numbers, be kind to yourself. Treat yourself with the same patience, care and understanding that you would extend to a loved one, who had the same score. If your score was in the higher numbers, keep building on what you are currently doing.

Breathing Space

Stop and relax for a moment. Feel your feet on the ground and the chair supporting your body. Follow your breath. Do not alter it; just observe it moving in and out. Do this a couple of times – and, then, stretch.

In the next section, we will look at how to enhance your resilience, using support networks.

Creating connections

The American Psychological Association has suggested the following strategies to increase your capacity for resilience:

- Prioritise relationships

- Join a group

- Take care of your body

- Practice mindfulness

- Avoid negative outlets

- Help others

- Be proactive

- Move toward your goals

- Look for opportunities for self-discovery

- Keep things in perspective

- Accept change

- Maintain a hopeful outlook

- Learn from your past

Humans are driven by a reciprocal desire to be seen, heard and understood. We also want to belong, in various ways. Numerous research studies have shown that having a good social support network is highly beneficial for our mental health.

Read the following story about finding connections – even in seemingly isolated situations.

Nicholas was a shy, 33-year-old freelance photographer, who attended a 'Writing for Self-Discovery' group at his community library.

He was born in the UK but emigrated to New Zealand with his family, when he was ten years old. In his late twenties, his world came crashing down around him and he decided to return to the UK.

Nicholas had been engaged to Stephanie and the couple were in the last stages of planning their wedding. When they had first met, four years previously, Nicholas was surprised that Stephanie was interested in someone like him. She was bubbly and lively; she came from what he considered to be a happy family. This was all so different from him and his own situation. Nicholas's father was an alcoholic, which meant that there had never been much money around; his father would spend it all on alcohol. Nicholas's mother tried her best, meanwhile, to protect her sons from their father's temper and abusive behaviour.

Nicholas often felt like he did not fit in; he described himself as a loner and 'the odd one out'. He hated conflict and would go out of his way to appease anyone else, rather than get involved in an argument. By observing his parents, Nicholas had seen how arguments escalated and vowed he would never behave in that way.

One day, after a week-long photoshoot, Nicholas arrived home earlier than planned. He was looking forward to seeing Stephanie and spending time with her. When he entered the house, however, he found his best friend, Jake, in a compromising position with his fiancée.

Nicholas was devastated. He could not understand what he had done wrong. Stephanie, tears flowing down her face, confessed that they had been having an affair – although only for a few weeks. Nicholas felt humiliated and experienced a deep sense of betrayal, from the two most important people in his life. As he was such a private man, his fiancée and best friend were the only people he would speak to about his problems. They had been the only ones he really trusted.

Stephanie was very apologetic and ended the affair with Jake. She wanted to continue her relationship with Nicholas and get married, but he decided it would be better if he moved out. He knew he could never trust her again.

Jake, on the other hand, did not apologise or even reach out to his best friend, which caused Nicholas a huge amount of pain. There were times when this loss felt even more devastating than the loss of his relationship with Stephanie.

Nicholas returned, reluctantly, to his parents' home. He threw himself into his work, to avoid thinking about everything that had gone wrong. After a few weeks, a job opportunity came up in the UK and Nicholas decided it was worth the risk to move countries. He returned to the UK for a fresh start.

When he arrived back, he was – understandably – still hurting. He did not feel he could trust anyone, nor that he had anyone in his life he could consider confiding in. Attending the 'Writing for Self-Discovery' group at his library, he nonetheless began to slowly develop and expand his support networks. Through writing tasks and discussions, he carefully considered his UK network – noting to himself those people whom he sensed he could trust. Nicholas was surprised to discover that there were, in fact, a couple of friends he could speak with, very honestly and openly. His old school friend Gemma, in particular, offered a listening ear and a sense of optimism. When Nicholas was struggling to cope with the overwhelming sadness and loss, from his life in New Zealand, he often felt the urge to isolate himself. His friendship with Gemma helped him to keep connecting, instead.

In the story you have just read, Nicholas managed to cope with his loss by reaching out to the people around him. In the next section, we will consider who you could talk to - particularly when you are experiencing difficulties, including a major crisis. You may feel the inclination to skip this exercise until you need support, but, knowing who you can contact, <u>before</u> life throws you a new challenge, can help to reduce the potential for anxiety. If you are worried about burdening or overwhelming one individual, then you could consider operating a rota system through aiming to have a range of people you can contact.

Developing your social support network

In this section, you will find a selection of ideas to help you in developing your support network. As you read through each suggestion, consider how it might work for you.

Go online

You might like to visit a networking site, such as *Meetup.com,* where you can find out about nearby face-to-face groups that are based on your own interests and hobbies. These groups offer a valuable opportunity to make and develop friendships, whilst doing an activity you enjoy.

Enrol in group exercise

Consider joining a physical or online exercise class. This is a great way to get yourself off the couch, to have fun, to be active and to improve both your mental resilience and fitness levels. Group exercise helps you achieve your physical and mental health goals, plus providing an opportunity to connect with people in your community.

Tap into your spiritual side

There is a growing body of research that suggests that spiritual beliefs and practices can have a powerful, positive impact on resilience levels. Opportunities to converse with a higher power, universal spirit or God - through regular practices like prayer and meditation - can give you hope, bring you comfort and help you feel more in control. You may also find that favourite passages from your holy book provide support during especially difficult times.

Perhaps you attend a nurturing church, synagogue, temple, mosque or other place of worship, on a regular basis. Or you may take yoga classes, attend a meditation group or undertake other spiritual practices where there are opportunities to mix with like-minded people. Whatever your beliefs, there will be either a local organisation/group, or online activity, to suit your spiritual needs.

Join a support group

You could consider joining a group, whether face to face or online, which speaks to your specific situation – for example, a bereavement support group or a rape survivors support group. As well as offering a chance to meet new people, these groups provide an opportunity for you to tell your story, alongside hearing other people's stories of coping and healing. Whilst your experience is unique, you can be comforted by people who can understand what you are going through.

That being said, timing can be crucial. You may not be ready to hear difficult and painful stories just yet. Wait until you feel strong enough or ready to share experiences with others. You will then, hopefully, discover for yourself that groups are invaluable sources of help and advice. They can also create opportunities for you to provide help and support, in return.

Volunteer

You may find that offering help in a more structured way – such as volunteering – allows you to develop your social network, while temporarily moving away from your own difficulties. Read about Amy's experiences of volunteering, in the following story:

> Amy attended her first 'Writing for Self-Discovery' workshop with her friend, Katy. A stay-at-home mum of two young children, Amy had lost her husband, Gary, to a heart attack five years previously.
>
> She struggled hugely with the loss of Gary, who had been her childhood sweet-heart. Amy could remember the day he died, so clearly. The couple had been saving up all year long, so they could take their daughters to Disneyland, Florida in the USA. This was to be their first holiday abroad as a family. On Gary's last day at work, before his annual leave started, he chatted happily about all the things they would do together. He kissed Amy goodbye – as he always did – and said, 'See you later, love. Don't forget to buy the suntan lotion.'
>
> A few hours later, Amy received a call from Gary's senior manager at the bus depot. Gary had collapsed and been taken to hospital. He had suffered from a heart attack. When Amy arrived at the accident and emergency department, the doctors told her they had been unable to save him.
>
> Amy was numb with shock. 'How?' she asked herself. Gary had been fit and healthy. It just did not make sense. She could not understand it.

Gary was her best friend and her soul mate. They were supposed to grow old together. She could not begin to imagine her life without him. Then her attention turned to the children. How was she going to tell the girls?

Amy had to learn quickly how to manage as a single parent. The early days were filled with an overwhelming sadness. She cried herself to sleep every night and could not see a point when things would get better. Each morning that she woke up without Gary, it was a struggle to get up and face the world. She would have stayed in bed if it had not been for her daughters.

Amy had plenty of support, initially. Over time, however, most of the visits stopped. Everyone got on with their own lives. That is, all but Amy's sister-in-law, Diane, who would drop in from time to time, and whose company Amy appreciated greatly. While chatting together one day, the subject of Gary's old clothes came up.

After much heartache, Amy decided it was time to donate Gary's old clothes to charity. When she arrived at the charity shop, she was welcomed by a shop worker, Katy, who was talkative and friendly – and who just seemed to understand her pain.

'If you ever want to have a chat, just pop in,' Katy offered.

One day, when Amy was feeling extremely low, she did just that. Katy realised that Amy had time on her hands during school hours and, so, asked her new friend if she would like to volunteer at the shop. Amy thought long and hard. She had no experience of this kind. She had never even worked before; Gary had been the breadwinner in their family. Eventually, though, she decided to give it a go, thinking that her efforts as a volunteer might help someone else.

Volunteering in the shop gave Amy a sense of purpose. It was a chance to develop new skills and boost her self-esteem, as she contributed to a worthy cause. Hearing her customers' stories of surviving and thriving, meanwhile, gave her hope that her own life could get better. Amy began to feel increasingly more positive, as she listened to others, rather than listening to her own negative thoughts – or 'cognitive distortions'*. Her negative thought patterns had been leading her to either minimise or catastrophise* her situation. Immersing herself in other people's stories helped her, instead, to put things in perspective.

Reflect on the opportunities for social support that we have covered so far and keep these in mind as you go through the next exercise. This is your chance to consider the sources of support in your own life.

- Complete the table that follows. I have filled in the first two rows as an example. Do add further rows and include your GP and any charitable organisations, who may also be able to help.

I could talk to/ I will contact	Relationship	Reason I will contact	Contact Details
Paula	Good friend	She is kind and compassionate – has experience of what I am going through.	07999 999 999
Samaritans	Organisation	Open 24 hours a day, 365 days a year. Can help when I am feeling low and in despair.	116 123 jo@samaritans.org

Remaining realistically hopeful is a crucial factor in sustaining resilience. It helps you to keep going, in spite of setbacks and difficulties. In her poem, *Hope Is The Thing With Feathers*, Massachusetts-born poet, Emily Dickinson, offers words of encouragement. She describes how hope '…perches in the soul' – and has kept so many warm.

Sophie, in her poem that follows, talks about hope as 'That little, tiny ray of light' which helped her to keep moving - one step at a time - once she left Manchester, after her relationship had ended.

That Little Ray of Light

1
It's happening
It's being overcome
Even though it's only the beginning

2
To take that step felt scary
Doing the step felt empowering; I loved Manchester

3
The sun is rising
There is finally some sort of light
That little tiny ray of light is all I need

4
Then I will be able to take another step
A bigger more resilient step
Closer to all of those rays

5
One day I will be able to dance
Dance with the sun!

Sophie
Inspired by Portia Nelson's poem, **Autobiography in Five Short Chapters**

Breathing Space

Stop and relax for a moment. Feel your feet on the ground and the chair supporting your body. Follow your breath; observe it moving in and out. Do this a couple of times and then stretch.

Resilience involves making choices and taking action

The following section focuses on the various actions you can take during times of change or difficulty.

Singer, actor and writer, Portia Nelson sums up her own life experiences in her poem *Autobiography in Five Short Chapters*, in which she brings to life the importance of making choices and taking action.

Autobiography in Five Short Chapters

1) I walk down the street.
There is a deep hole in the sidewalk.
I fall in.
I am lost... I am hopeless.
It isn't my fault.
It takes forever to find a way out.

2) I walk down the same street.
There is a deep hole in the sidewalk.
I pretend I don't see it.
I fall in again.
I can't believe I'm in the same place.
But it isn't my fault.
It still takes a long time to get out.

3) I walk down the same street.
There is a deep hole in the sidewalk.
I see it is there.
I still fall in... it's a habit.
My eyes are open.
I know where I am.
It is my fault.
I get out immediately.

4) I walk down the same street.
There is a deep hole in the sidewalk.
I walk around it.

5) I walk down another street.

Portia Nelson
From **There's a Hole in My Sidewalk: The Romance of Self-Discovery** by Portia Nelson.
Copyright © 1993 by Portia Nelson. Reprinted with the permission of Beyond Words/Atria Books,
a division of Simon & Schuster, Inc. All rights reserved.

In her poem, Nelson describes walking down a street and falling into a hole. This soon becomes a habit. After a number of attempts to avoid the hole, she eventually breaks the habit by walking down another street.

Have you ever 'fallen into a hole' because of a habit? What did you do to pull yourself out? Did you take action or did you hope it would all go away?

Burying your head in the sand may be a strategy you use when dealing with difficulties or addressing particular problems and may help in the short term. To save trouble in the future, however, and increase your resilience, it is important to take action as soon as you can do so. Tackling a problem head on might seem difficult at first, but writing down details of the situation in a journal, or notebook, can help you move towards decisive action.

Let us try with that now, in completing the following exercise:

- Write about a problem or habit you are currently tackling, including as much detail as possible

- List the reasons you consider this situation to be a problem

- Write down all the solutions that come to mind

- List the pros and cons of taking each particular course of action

- Look closely over your list of pros and cons. Write down which course of action feels the most likely to solve – or help with – your problem

- Complete the following sentence stem:

The reason this course of action is the best one to take…

- If relevant, consider the most useful time to take this action; write the date down.

If you are still unsure, or if the course of action above does not instinctively feel right, then try 'sleeping on it'. Provided the deadline for taking action is not imminent, put the list aside for a couple of days, before you add to it again.

Breathing Space

Use '**3-2-1**'. Look around you. Notice three things you can see and two things you can hear. Now take one, deep, cleansing breath.

On the next page, we are going to explore your patterns of resilience through the various stages of your life.

River of Life

We have all had to overcome a major difficulty or life-changing event, at some point in time. You may have moved to another part of the country, been a victim of crime or 'come out' to family and friends. We reach a point, inevitably, where we acknowledge that life will never be the same again.

Some of you may be familiar with the 'River of Life'. This is a narrative and visual tool, often used by social workers to help children and young people tell their life stories, using the metaphor* of a river.

We are about to look closely at your story so far, highlighting those pivotal moments where your life – or your 'river' – has experienced twists and turns. It may have been calm sometimes but, at other times, fast-flowing. Your river may have encountered rocks, or obstacles, and changed direction. You can dive in at the deep end with this, or start where you prefer. For example, 'I went to secondary school'; 'I was diagnosed with cancer'; 'I went to prison'; 'I became a wheelchair user'; 'My parents separated'; 'I got married' – and so on.

Let us take a look at the key transitions in your life, through the next exercise. This involves using Post-it notes, which are great for containing your emotions and keeping your writing brief.

- Select eleven Post-it notes and then identify eleven key transitions in your life. Write down one key transition per Post-it note; an initial, start point transition has been completed for you, already below, so you will complete a set of twelve transitions in all. Aim to use a maximum of five words for each transition. Your transitions can be either positive or negative. Write them down randomly, to begin with, then place them in chronological order, afterwards.

Start with:

1. I was born.

2. ....

3. ....

4. ....

5. ....

6. ....

7. ....

8. ....

9. ....

10. ....

11. ....

12. ....

- Read your key transitions aloud. Try to connect with your story, as you do so.

- Pause for a moment, now, so you can look at your key transitions; note down any patterns and emotions which rise to the surface, as you do this.

I invite you, at this point, to 'sit with' your emotions for a short while. Allow them to be present, without judging, or trying to change them.

Being human is to experience both, so-called 'comfortable' and 'uncomfortable' feelings. Your task is to become familiar with these feeling states and work through them, rather than avoid them. By sitting with your feelings, you can develop distress-tolerance skills. Rumi, a Persian poet and Sufi master born in 1207, gives us a strategy for this, in his poem 'The Guest House', featured in *Rumi: Selected Poems,* translated by Coleman Barks with John Moyne (Penguin, 2004).

The poem advises us to invite our feelings in and to entertain all of them – from joy to sorrow – as if they were guests in our home. This is sound advice. Embracing, examining and clarifying your emotions – whatever they may be – will help you to build your resilience.

After sitting with your emotions as your guests, if necessary, carry out a self-care activity, before continuing with this next section.

- Look carefully, now, at the key transitions you identified in the previous exercise. Pay attention to all the transitions that made it on to your list. Is there a transition missing? What do you notice about the way you have arranged your Post-it notes? Does anything jump out at you? Write for ten minutes.

- What do you notice about the positive transitions?

Breathing Space

Pause to appreciate your hard work, so far. Allow yourself to take a deep breath, have a yawn and stretch your limbs.

In the next exercise, we are going to explore your life transitions from a new perspective.

Changing voices

Writing about yourself in the third person, using pronouns such as 'he', 'she' or 'they', can be quite an eye-opener. It is a useful way to put distance between you and your experiences, allowing space for new insights.

- Look over your transitions list again and choose one transition that you wish to examine more closely. Perhaps you will choose the least emotional one, or the quickest and easiest. You may well opt for the one you instinctively need to explore. Write about that transition in detail, including your thoughts and feelings. Remember, this may be the point where you need that box of tissues I mentioned, back in the first chapter. You might feel emotional if you are opening old wounds or celebrating happy memories.

- Write about yourself, for ten minutes, in the third person. Complete this sentence stem:

- Her/His/Their life changed direction when…

- Read over your work and complete the following sentence stem:

When I read this, I am aware…

Breathing Space

Take a well-deserved break. Finish the rest of this exercise later.

How I coped

Now, let's continue to examine your life transitions. This time, we will focus on the skills that helped you to cope.

- Referring to your transitions, without judgement, can you identify how you coped in the face of adversity or change? Include both helpful and unhelpful coping skills. For example, a helpful coping skill might be to talk about your worries to a friend, to a trusted family member, or to a counsellor or teacher. An unhelpful coping skill may be to 'bottle things up' or 'drown your sorrows', in drinking excessive amounts of alcohol. What specific skills did you use? List them.

- Reflect on the skills in your list that are no longer helpful to you. Write down your thoughts.

- Out of all the skills you listed previously, which ones could you use in going forward, when new obstacles or difficulties come your way? Write for ten minutes.

Now that you have finished working through this chapter, review the writing you have done and complete the following sentence stem:

- The main insight I gained from this chapter…

Take a moment, now, to acknowledge all your hard work.

Finally, if you would like a reminder, at any point, about the skills required to become more resilient, you may wish to refer to Carolyn's poem, below.

Landed

An innocent,
Absorbing everything,
Bobbing on the waves.

A deep cut,
Dark wound,
Sinking through the ocean,
Rock bottom.
Numb. Floating slowly back up.
Drifting on the raft,
Tending the sails,
Bailing out water,
Watching for land,
In and out of ports.

Landing, building, bonding,
Tending the inner fires,
Nurturing inner strength,
Feeding courage, love,
Inner.

Branching out,
Venturing forth, but always returning to the ocean,
Looking for the wreckage
Searching through the flotsam,
Sinking, floating,
Disorientated,
Returning again and again to land.
Struggling up the beach,

Back and forth,
Brick
by
Brick.
Driftwood, by driftwood.
Perseverance.
Determination.
Hope.
Faith.
Acceptance.
Courage.
Wonderment.
Landed.

Carolyn

To sum up...

- Resilience is the capacity to positively adapt, during - or following - significant adversity.

- Support networks are crucial for instilling and reminding us of the importance of realistic hope.

- Strengthening resilience after adversity is achievable. It is vital that you identify effective coping strategies.

In the next chapter, we will examine your values and establish how to rebuild your personal identity, after overcoming adversity.

Chapter 3

Building a personal identity

Identity is the role you chose to play in the story of the Universe.
Maria V. Shall

Have you ever paused and asked yourself the question: 'Who am I?' Was the question difficult to answer? What did your honest answers reveal? Did they surprise you?

The writing task that follows allows you to explore this question, now, by inviting you to list the facts that describe you. I use this exercise frequently, as a warm-up, in poetry therapy groups. I have noticed that participants are often surprised by what they have written or – indeed – omitted. Some people list their family role(s), career(s), ethnicity, religion, nationality, life purpose or specific issues.(e.g.,health challenges). There are no right or wrong answers. I encourage you to write instinctively, noting down whatever comes to mind just allow thoughts to flow through your pen. Set a timer and complete your list in two minutes.

- Complete the following sentence stem:

The facts that describe me…

- List your answers. Be sure to finish when the timer sounds.

- Look over your list. Does anything on your list surprise you, or seem particularly interesting?

- Write about the most significant fact on your list.

- Read over what you have written and complete the following sentence stem:

When I read this, I notice or am surprised to find…

What did you notice about your writing? What did the facts about you reveal? Were you surprised that, perhaps, you did not mention your job or your role as a parent, or the colour of your skin? Did you notice that you put a significant fact a long way down on your list? Discovering and reconnecting with what is important to you can help you appreciate yourself, as well as to carve out the role you will play in the story of the universe.

Identity is not static. How we identify ourselves changes – for example, as we get older. Over time, the conditions we live under tend to alter. We might go through a number of adverse experiences, such as overcoming the effects of trauma, the loss of a loved one or pet, or going through a divorce or separation. Each of these can bring about a change in our identity.

Such changes can influence and alter the way we operate in the world. It is important to clarify whether the way we identify our 'self' helps or hinders our ability to be resilient.

In the story that follows, read about Jenny, who took the chance to re-examine her beliefs and identity, after overcoming serious illness.

> *Jenny was a high-flying solicitor, who worked for a busy firm in the city and had three adult children. Being diagnosed with breast cancer, at the age of fifty-five, shook the very foundation of her identity. She was forced to reconsider her beliefs about what mattered in life.*
>
> *When Jenny found a lump in her breast, initially, she had expected her GP to say it was nothing to worry about. After tests, however, she was horrified to find out she had early-stage breast cancer.*
>
> *Jenny struggled with the diagnosis, at first, fearing she would die. She worried about her children and also had to reassure her new partner, George. He had handled the news badly and Jenny hid how terrified she was, a lot of the time.*
>
> *Once Jenny had been able to digest the information, gradually, and talk to her close friends and family, she decided she could beat the cancer. She promised herself, meanwhile, that she would try to enjoy every moment with her family.*

Surgery – and several bouts of chemotherapy – left her exhausted. Jenny hated being vulnerable and having to rely on her family to do the chores and provide support; this was a role she had previously loved. But she did her best to focus on getting better.

Once the cancer was in remission, Jenny knew it was time to rebuild her life. Determined to stay fit and healthy, she began walking around her local area, as a form of gentle exercise. She later joined a walking group, which eventually led to her taking part in a 5K run, for cancer research. Jenny felt a real sense of achievement. She would never have considered doing this before she had been diagnosed with cancer; she just wouldn't have had the courage.

When it came to her career, Jenny decided she wanted to do something that was more in tune with her values. Being forced to contemplate death had pushed her to consider how she wanted to live – and who she wanted to be. She gave up her job as a solicitor and began working at her local, city farm. She had always loved animals and yearned to work with them when she was younger, but as a university student, had decided to follow her parents' footsteps into law. Now, she had the chance to follow her real passion!

Although it had been a difficult time for Jenny and her family, recovering from cancer helped her to focus on – in her words – 'What really matters'. Jenny's priorities changed and she carved out a new identity, one that was much more appreciative of herself, her family and her relationships.

Jenny was pushed to re-evaluate her beliefs – those thoughts and ideas that she held up as true and accurate. In turn, these beliefs had an impact on her identity.

When there is a change in your circumstances, your beliefs, roles and responsibilities may vary, too. Your relationship with yourself and others will inevitably, also, take on different forms. Remember, finally, that re-examining your beliefs, values and priorities can help you to identify the role you will choose to play in your part of the story of the universe.

Discovering your values

Our values stem from our beliefs and operate generally in the background. Being clear about your values – what you hold dear and consider to be valuable – improves your self-awareness. This increases the chances of you accomplishing your goals and making better decisions, since you understand what genuinely motivates you.

We are now going to reflect on your values, with the help of an imaginary best friend. Give yourself plenty of time for this exercise, knowing that it is worth putting in the effort to identify your values – that they are essential to your future happiness and success.

When you were a child, perhaps you had a best friend whom you completely trusted – someone who was great company and always there for you. If not, you may have still longed for such a friend. Given the opportunity, now, to choose a best friend, what qualities would you seek? What values would that person hold? Give yourself the freedom to pick any quality or value, rather than focusing on an existing friend's attributes. The values listed below are some examples:

Love
Learning
Stability
Honesty
Freedom
Fun
Happiness
Adventure
Dependability
Open-mindedness
Security
Peace
Decisive
Health
Eco-friendliness
Creativity
Compassion
Respect
Spirituality
Optimism
Responsibility

Safety
Success
Wisdom
Faith
Pleasure
Reliability
Loyalty
Efficiency
Commitment
Popularity
Self-reliance
Boldness
Justice
Independence
Prosperity
Variety
Reputation
Spontaneity
Intuition
Sharing
Education

- Create a list of qualities for your imaginary best friend and explain why each quality matters to you.

- Write a list of the values that matter most to you, in your life. Try to aim for ten items.

- Now look back over your list of values and choose the top six that you feel you must honour in your life.

- Reflect on your top six values and complete the following sentence stem:

When I read the list of my top six values, I am aware…

Compare the list of qualities for your imaginary best friend, with your own list of values. You may find that you have the same, or similar, values. Often the values you look for in others are the ones you hold dear. Your top six are usually described as your 'core values'. These are qualities that naturally feel important to you. They are essential factors to consider when looking for a job, choosing your life-long partner, finding new friends, engaging in health and fitness, or setting and achieving your goals.

Breathing Space

Pause to appreciate your hard work. Allow yourself to take a deep breath, have a yawn and stretch your limbs.

Setting goals

In this next activity, I will invite you to turn your chosen values into actions.

- Spend a few moments looking over your core values list, then go through the list and rate each value on a scale of 0-10, according to how much it matters to you ('0' being the least important and '10' being extremely important).

- Now, identify two values on your list that you do not seem to be honouring. For example, one of your values may be 'staying healthy', but you have not engaged in regular exercise or have been overindulging in fast foods and/or alcohol.

- Choose one value to work with and answer the following questions:

  - What would help me to honour this value and truly embrace it as part of my daily life?

  - What actions could I take to help me in the short term and long term?

- Write down a date and time when you will take those actions.

You may have now recognised the actions you can take, to honour some of your core values. Choose another value that you do not seem to be honouring and work through the questions above.

Managing expectations

During your lifetime, you will inevitably come across people in your circle who do not share all of your values. Reflect on this as you read the story that follows.

Lauren, a 24-year-old freelance marketer, came from a small village in the north of England. After graduating from university, she moved to London. A few years later, she started seeing a counsellor as she was having trouble maintaining friendships and romantic relationships. Her initial sessions focused on friendships. Lauren was troubled by a particular event that had taken place, recently and shared it with her counsellor.

Lauren had arranged to meet with her friend Karen at their favourite coffee shop. They had got to know each other, initially, when Lauren first moved to London, but had not seen one other for a while. Lauren arrived early, as usual. She came from a family who insisted on punctuality; it had been drummed into her that you should always arrive early to any meeting. Lauren felt quite anxious being on her own and – also as usual – Karen arrived fifteen minutes late. Karen did not bother to apologise and Lauren felt upset there was no hint of remorse.

Even though Lauren enjoyed seeing her friend that day, inside, she was quietly seething. She felt resentful and could not seem to let it go. Punctuality was a value that Lauren cherished. Surely, her friend should know that, by now. Karen, on the other hand, had never seen punctuality as an issue, particularly amongst friends.

She took a relaxed attitude to most things in life and was unaware that Lauren was upset. After all, Lauren hadn't mentioned anything. Why should there be an issue?

Lauren came away from the encounter feeling disappointed and frustrated. In the past, she would have held on to those feelings and they would have surfaced as an angry comment, or action, at a later date. This time, however, after exploring the issue with her counsellor, Lauren plucked up the courage to have an honest and respectful conversation with Karen. She decided to share how she was feeling.

Getting things 'off her chest' in this way enabled Lauren to enjoy a more genuine relationship with her friend. She was also able to accept that Karen's attitude to punctuality was part of her own identity and not a lack of respect for their friendship.

Through the process of counselling, Lauren made a connection with how she reacted in her friendships and romantic relationships. Just as she had done with Karen, she always assumed that her partners shared the same set of values and she judged their actions accordingly. In time, she began to forgive many of the perceived 'offences' from past relationships. This helped her to release the hurt she'd been holding onto and move forward with a happier future.

Judging someone by our own set of values is very common. From my own counselling work, I know of many examples where people have been surprised and offended because another person did not behave in the same way they would have done. This is often because, either, that other person does not share the same values, or the particular value in question is not a core value for them. With this in mind, it is important that we communicate our values, manage our expectations and acknowledge that we are all living out our own set of values, through life.

Discerning your character

You are now, hopefully more aware of how important it is to recognise and communicate your values. In the sections that follow, you will have the opportunity to explore your identity in more detail. This will help you to understand yourself more clearly and, in turn, have greater control over your thoughts and behaviour.

In the first instance, we are about to delve into your character using metaphors*. You may be familiar with metaphors already, and you might have noticed that we began working with them when we wrote in response to 'Resilience', the poem by Paulette Brooks in Chapter 2.

Metaphors are hugely symbolic and can be playful. They may have several layers, reveal deeper truths and provide opportunities to discover, reflect and rebuild your identity. For that reason, we will continue to work with them throughout this book. Have a look at Emma's example, through her poem, below.

Emma is a survivor of domestic abuse*, who attended my 'Working With Your Inner Critic' therapeutic writing workshop, in which she was invited to describe herself as a piece of furniture. That piece of furniture became a metaphor for her personality.

Chair

I am a chair.
I am relatively new but have been slightly weathered.
There are faint shoe prints from people who have stood on me rather than sat, but I am sturdy and have not been broken.
My legs are slightly loose but all they need is a bit of tightening and I'll be 100% sturdy again.
I have been a support for many people and will be for many to come.
I have a soft cushion and I give people comfort; wherever there is a scruff mark it can be wiped off.
I hope to last many years even if I need to occasionally be repaired, or cleaned or replace my cushion.
I have the ground that supports my four sturdy legs,
And it will never fail me because there is balance in my structure.
When I am old and used up you will see the history on my surface; the wood will be darkened and worn, but it will show my character – and that I will cherish.

Emma

Now it is your turn to experiment with using a metaphor to describe yourself. Imagine yourself as one of the following:

- A piece of furniture
- An item of clothing
- The weather
- A vegetable

- Write about yourself as that item or element. Highlight your strengths, talents, abilities, achievements and the ways in which you overcame adversity. Write for fifteen minutes.

- Now re-read what you have written and complete the following sentence stem:

I realise…

Breathing Space

Stop and relax for a moment. Feel your feet on the ground and the chair supporting your body. Follow your breath; observe it moving in and out. Do this a couple of times and, then, stretch.

Carving out a new identity

After experiencing adversity, your confidence and sense of self can be weakened or fragile – as in Jenny's example, at the beginning of the chapter. Perhaps this became more obvious to you, in the last exercise. Now is the time to start rebuilding your sense of identity. While this process may take a while, your confidence levels can – and will – improve.

Everyone finds their own path on this journey of self-discovery. For some people, it might include going on a pilgrimage to seek answers to life's big questions – to discover who they are, what they want and why they are here. Victoria Field – the writer and poetry therapist – did just that. She documented the experience in her authentic and compelling book, *Baggage: A Book of Leavings*.

Field describes, in that text, her struggles and triumphs in an open and intimate manner. They include the end of her first marriage and the 212-mile pilgrim journey that she took, walking along the Camino de Santiago to reach the shrine of St James, in North West Spain. This popular pilgrimage has helped many people to find answers to their questions and establish a new identity and stronger sense of self.

A journey like this is not suitable for everyone, of course. Duke, a resident at Her Majesty's Prison Risley (HMP Risley), did not have the freedom to embark on a physical journey. Nevertheless, he was able to use his time in prison to consider the question, 'Why am I here?'

An interesting suggestion is made in the following quote, often attributed to writer Mark Twain: 'The two most important days in your life are the day you are born and the day you find out why.'

Reflect on this, as you read the poem that follows.

Why Am I Here?

Why am I here?
Is the question I asked myself
One day when I was sitting alone in my cell
Is it to gain wealth
Maintain good health
Or to retain stealth?
To blend in with everybody else
To do what society tells you to do?
What might not be for me could be for you
But why am I really here is the question
And the answer isn't so clear.
Am I here to inform others that the world is flat?
Even though some say that's a load of crap
Some then claim to know it's a sphere
Is it to hear the cheers of peers
Or to capitalise on capital through a multitude of careers?
Am I here to be the voice for those who are afraid to speak
To be the strong for the weak
To be the shepherd not the sheep
Or to wake those who are asleep?
Am I here by mistake or out of love?
Am I here through making a mistake or just because?
Am I here by accident or on purpose?
Am I here to find a purpose?
Am I here to inspire before I expire?

Don't think you can't reach for the stars, go to Mars
Then reach even higher
Whatever your priors.
Am I here to be a messiah?
Am I here to ignite the fire that lies within
In everybody
Her and him?
Why am I here in this world of sin?
Why am I here with this bottle of gin?
Why am I here, not my next of kin?
Why am I here, I don't know where to begin.

Duke
Resident, Her Majesty's Prison Risley

In his poem, Duke contemplates whether he is a 'shepherd' or a 'sheep'. Is he, perhaps, a voice for those who cannot speak? He concludes the poem with admitting that he does not know where to begin.

As you embark on your own voyage of self-discovery, you can begin by asking yourself some key questions, to help you figure out who you are and why you are here.

For the following exercise, write whatever comes to mind, without censoring. Just go straight ahead with your first thoughts:

- What makes me different and unique from others? Write for seven minutes.

- What is my purpose? Why am I really here, on this earth?

- What am I passionate about?

- When I look closely in the mirror, do I love what I see? Why is this the case?

- How can I 'ignite the fire that lies within'?

- Read over your responses and complete this sentence stem:

Now that I have read what I have written, I feel…

Breathing Space

Pause to appreciate your hard work. Allow yourself to take a deep breath, have a yawn and stretch your limbs.

Identity and confidence

You have started to identify the ways in which you stand out from the crowd. Were your answers from the previous exercise revealing? From time to time, repeat the exercise and note down any significant or subtle changes.

Confidence is crucial. It is an attitude that many of us strive for. When you are confident, you feel good about who you are and are more upbeat. You take risks, trust your instincts, and – ultimately – make better decisions.

Confidence and resilience are closely related. Every positive experience of coping enhances your confidence and self-esteem. So, the more resilient you become, the more confident you are. In turn, the more confident you become, the more resilient you are; the two go hand in hand.

- Reflect, in your writing, on what confidence means to you. Write instinctively and continue for three minutes.

How did you find the exercise? The *New Little Oxford Dictionary* defines confidence as, 'A positive feeling gained from a belief in your own ability to do things well'. Confidence can be a thought, feeling or attitude. We often gain confidence when we have *taken action*, rather than before.

Sometimes, you can lack confidence in one particular area of your life and, then, mistakenly describe yourself as someone who 'lacks confidence generally'. It is important to challenge this.

The great news is, if you are confident in one area of your life, you can transfer the skills, thoughts and attitudes to any other area of life. The key is to identify those positive skills, thoughts and attitudes.

A question I ask, at my confidence-building workshops – and one that inevitably creates a lively discussion – is, 'What is your best feature?' Clarification is usually requested at this point. For example, am I referring to something aesthetic, or in terms of character qualities? Either way, it may (or may not) surprise some readers to know that, even after plenty of time debating this matter, some people experience much discomfort and find they simply cannot share their best feature. Many of us, at some point during our lifetime, have learnt that it is not okay to share the best or positive aspects of ourselves. It is often seen as arrogant.

My workshops take a vastly different turn, however, if I ask a group, 'What is your worst feature?' There is usually no need for clarification! A long list is generated, immediately – well before I have an opportunity to interject. We are far more eager, it seems, to share the negative aspects of ourselves. Is this true for you?

- 'What is your best feature and why?' Write it down.

Think about how you felt when answering that question. Did you feel uncomfortable? Did you manage to write down your best feature? Were you hesitant, or did you start comparing yourself with others, in your mind? It is important to make a note of your process and thoughts and then challenge any negative beliefs.

- Write down how you felt, when asked to write about your best feature.

Shining your light

We live in a world where sharing our successes might mean, unfortunately, being called conceited or self-important. Sometimes we 'play small', so that other people do not feel insecure around us. The truth is that playing small can, however, have a huge impact on your confidence and self-esteem. When we have been accustomed to playing small, we often struggle to be positive and confident. This has a knock-on effect when it comes to our resilience levels. A great exercise to help us stay confident and resilient is to remind ourselves of the positive things about ourselves.

- Start a list of positive things about you, now.

    - Put the list aside for a couple of weeks, knowing that you will add to it again.

    - Keep going like this, across fortnightly intervals, until you reach 100 positive things on your list.

Positive affirmations

We are now going to look at an effective tool that will help you to develop a healthier and more positive view of yourself. As an added bonus, this versatile approach can also be used to help you get through tough times.

A positive affirmation is a sentence that describes a desired situation and is repeated many times. On the following page are a few examples:

I can get through this.
I deserve love and happiness.
I am feeling more confident.

The word 'affirmation' comes from the verb 'to affirm', one meaning of which is 'to state as a fact'. Positive affirmations are wonderful tools to help us cope with the challenges that life throws our way and the negative messages we send ourselves. They help us reprogramme our thinking, which is particularly useful if we regularly take part in negative self-talk.

To help make affirmations as effective as possible, try to connect with your senses and repeat your affirmations with intention. It may seem strange initially, voicing and repeating those positive affirmations. You may not truly believe them, at first, however, it is worth persevering.

Part of the power behind positive affirmations lies in repeating the phrases over and over. If you tell yourself something often enough, sooner or later you will believe it. This same principle is used by advertisers, when aiming to convince people about the value of their products.

Once you create a habit with affirmations, and are committed to staying with the process, you will be able to notice the profound difference positive affirmations can bring about – in your thoughts, your behaviour and, ultimately, your resilience. They are particularly effective when completed as part of a wider journey of self-discovery, such as the one you are going through, with this book.

You affirm and create your life experiences

Affirmations work both ways. At some point in your life, you have probably used affirmations without knowing it – although, almost certainly, in a negative way! Is there something you say to yourself on a regular basis that is not particularly kind? A scenario that has come up in the women's groups I have run over the years involves accidently spilling a drink. Participants have at times, when they have spilt some tea or coffee, their immediate reaction has been to say, 'I am so stupid!'

Spilling a drink in this situation is obviously an accident. If you repeatedly call yourself 'stupid', however, you may encourage others to do the same and it will eventually become a self-fulfilling prophecy.

Whatever your own negative affirmations might be, try not to be so hard on yourself! An accident such as spilling a drink might be annoying, but it should not be an excuse to speak harshly to yourself. It is essential that we train our minds to be kinder and more compassionate towards ourselves. This will help us to see other aspects of our lives in more positive ways and deal with challenges more effectively.

In the next exercise, you will design your own positive affirmation. Using your own words is important, when creating your affirmation. As Mary Beth Williams comments in *The PTSD Workbook*,
(New Harbinger, 2002), 'Affirmations are a form of positive self-talk that can state how you really
want to see yourself and your body. Thus, you are the best person to create your own affirmations.'

To get started, think of a situation where you may need a more positive frame of mind.
Perhaps you are about to give a presentation and are feeling anxious, for instance. Or maybe
you would like to feel more confident when you look in the mirror, as another example. Whatever
the specific issue or situation, use the guidelines that follow, to help you create your positive
affirmation. You may need to try this exercise out a few times, before you come up with an affirmation that feels instinctively right for you.

Guidelines for writing a positive affirmation

- Keep it:

  - **Personal** - Make it personal by using 'I' or 'My'.

  - **Present tense** - Use the present tense. Write as if you already have the quality you
    desire – For example, 'I am confident', rather than, 'I will be confident' - otherwise, it
    will always be a future promise.

  - **Positive** - Use positive words and phrases that feel comfortable to you. Describe
    exactly what you want, rather than what you do not want. For example, 'I am success-
    ful', rather than, 'I am not a failure'.

  - **Realistic** - There may be times when a positive statement feels so far from your true
    experience that you are unable to believe it. In such cases, it is helpful to include
    words that show you are moving towards your ultimate goal. For example, you might
    prefer to say, 'I am becoming stronger', rather than, 'I am strong'. Or 'I am trying my
    best', rather than, 'I am at my best'.

  - **Succinct -** Try not to overcomplicate things by packing too much into one affirmation,
    or by using extra words unnecessarily. Keep it simple (for the time being).

- Write out a first version of your positive affirmation.

- Read your words aloud. Do they feel right to you? Is your affirmation personal, in the present tense, positive, realistic and succinct?

- Make any changes to your words, as necessary.

- When you have finished, write out a final version of your positive affirmation and put it in a place where you can refer to it, easily.

Remember to read your positive affirmation aloud, with conviction, several times a day. Placing your words somewhere you will see them may help. You could use your positive affirmation as a screensaver or set a reminder on your mobile phone, to repeat your affirmation throughout the day.

You may wish to write out your positive affirmation by hand, on a regular basis, too. As Mary Beth Williams comments, the physical act of writing can '…help an affirmation to become a habit of thought, a new self-message that you have incorporated into yourself and made a part of your belief system'. Consider writing out your affirmation a few times first thing, each morning, or at night, just before you go to sleep.

Now that you have finished working through this chapter, review the writing you have done and complete the following sentence stem:

- The main insight I gained from this chapter…

Take a moment, now, to acknowledge all your hard work.

Finally, if you need a reminder at any point about what it means to have a strong sense of identity, you may like to refer to Nicky's poem, below.

Woman

What does it mean to be, well, Me
a woman
with a few silver threads
weaving through my hair
like a fine spiders' web?
my locks hold the knowledge of heartache
addiction
happier times
& love

my eyes take in the world around me
at times i can fill up buckets
with liquid stories pouring down my face

there is so much wrong with this world
that i keep a roll of loving tape
so i can mend my heart
every time it breaks
i'm not yet a mother, or a wife
but i am somebody's daughter
somebody's sister
somebody's friend

there are lines etched into my body
some earned
some designed
a canvas...telling the story of my life
i'm a dancer to the beat of my drum
a poet - speaker of my own words

all women have many different tales to tell
i can only tell you the tale of me

i breathe
i believe
& i dream

Nicky Smit

To sum up...

- Identity is fluid, and adverse experiences can change us. Honouring your values can bring a real sense of purpose and meaning to your life.

- When confident, we tend to feel positive about ourselves and life in general. It enables us to deal with life's ups and downs more effectively.

- Words are powerful. Speak loving and kind words to yourself.

In the next chapter, we will concentrate on how you can live more harmoniously with your inner critic. We will look at how to prevent the inner critic from sabotaging your opportunities, so that you can experience a more fulfilling and happier life.

Chapter 4

Working with the inner critic

Change your thoughts and you change your world.
Norman Vincent Peale

Awareness is the first step towards change

Think back to a time when you stepped out of your comfort zone to carry out a challenging activity. Perhaps you auditioned for a part in a local play, finally completed that job application, or walked into a networking event and worked the room.

If you managed to *just do it*, without hesitation, you were probably listening to your supportive and positive inner voice – your *inner coach* – the one that tells you, 'You can do this. It may be a challenge at first, but you've got it covered.'

If you struggled, or made several attempts and failed, because you told yourself that you were not good enough, you were probably listening to your *inner critic*.

The inner critic is the voice that judges, shames and condemns us, making us feel inadequate. It is the voice that sows seeds of doubt. It feeds us negative messages, such as, 'No one will want to hear what you have to say. You are so boring. You don't deserve this…'. These critical messages often involve comparing ourselves less favourably with others. The inner critic is that little – or sometimes loud – voice in your head, which prevents you from taking action and achieving your dreams.

It is essential that you become aware of – and recognise – the voice of your inner critic, to prevent it from affecting your confidence and resilience. In this chapter we will examine your inner critic, carefully, to help you understand its role, function and logic.

You may well notice that the inner critic's power shifts into a higher gear, as you begin to focus on it. For that reason, we will concentrate first on enhancing your positive self-image – a key aspect of building and maintaining resilience.

What is in a name?

We will begin with enhancing self-image by using an acrostic of your name. In an acrostic, the letters of a word or phrase are written vertically down the page, with each letter beginning a new line. The acrostic may feature your first name, a nickname/pet name, your last name or even your full name. In this exercise, you are going to write something positive about yourself for each letter.

You may wish to follow my example below to get started. If you get stuck, you could think of words that other people have used to describe you. Play around with the words. They might describe who you are, what you do or how you act. The key here is to say only positive things about yourself.

My Acrostic
Charitable
Happy
Attentive
Reliable
Motivating
Authentic
Inspiring
Nurturing
Energetic

- Now it is your turn. Write your name vertically down the page. For each letter, write something positive about yourself. You may write one word, or several words, on each line.

- Once you have finished your acrostic, read it aloud. Then complete the following sentence stem:

When I am called [insert the name you used to create your acrostic] I feel…

Do remember that, as you begin to challenge the inner critic, its voice will become much louder. However, *you* have the power to challenge that voice and the opinions it offers you.

Facing the inner critic

Did you manage to find plenty of positive words to complete your acrostic? Or did your inner critic raise its head? This next exercise will help you recognise the ways in which the inner critic manifests itself, and the impact it has, on different aspects of your life.

- Set a timer and spend three minutes writing down a list of things that your inner critic says. Be honest with yourself. Be specific. Finish when the timer sounds.

- Look over your list. What does your inner critic specifically prevent you from doing, being or achieving? List those activities or achievements.

- Write about the most significant activity, or achievement, from your list above. Write for ten minutes.

Breathing Space

Stop and relax for a moment. Feel your feet on the ground and the chair supporting your body. Follow your breath; observe it moving in and out. Do this a couple of times and then stretch.

Examining the external critics in your life

You will, by now, no doubt be starting to recognise the often destructive and negative impact the inner critic has, on your experiences. The inner critic is your own voice. With that in mind, you may wonder about the reasons why you continue to punish yourself – perhaps even unconsciously – and sabotage your success. Where does this critical voice come from?

The inner critic often starts life as an external critic. It can stem from remarks made by people in authority, when you were younger – such as teachers, priests, carers, parents, or other members of your family.

In a moment, we will complete an exercise that involves writing in response to a poem. Firstly, let's take a look at the poem itself, which is called *Marks* by Linda Pastan, an American poet of Jewish background, who was the former poet laurate of Maryland (1991-1995). This poem is featured in her book *The Five Stages of Grief.*

Marks

My husband gives me an A
for last night's supper,
an incomplete for my ironing,
a B plus in bed.
My son says I am average,
an average mother, but if
I put my mind to it
I could improve.
My daughter believes
in Pass/Fail and tells me
I pass. Wait 'til they learn
I'm dropping out.

Linda Pastan

Writing in response to a poem

Now is your chance to respond to Pastan's poem. Read the poem again, slowly –if possible, read it aloud, to feel the words in your mouth and get a sense of the poem's rhythms and beats. Pay attention to any emotions or memories it stirs in you. As you answer the questions that follow, imagine that you are telling a friend about your reaction to the poem.

- Where do you see yourself in the poem, when you read *Marks* by Linda Pastan,?

- What could you improve if you put your mind to it?

- Identify a word, phrase or line in the poem that you feel connected to, or that you feel is calling for your attention.

- Using your chosen word, phrase or line as a prompt, write for six minutes.

- Read over your last piece of writing and complete the following sentence stem:

Now that I have read what I have written, I notice or am surprised to find…

Looking back over the poem, we can see Pastan describing how her family members give her marks for the various roles she plays in their lives. From an early age, we are assessed by – and compared with – others.

Have you ever been likened to a sibling, cousin or friend? As a child, you may have heard phrases such as, 'You are not like John. He is so much better at…', or, 'If only you could look like Shania. She is much more…'.

Read the following story about how comments such as these can affect a person's life for years to come.

> Jamie was a handsome, single man in his late twenties who had recently landed his dream contract in the music industry. He had been made responsible for talent scouting and overseeing the development of recording artists, at a well-respected record label. It was a role he had worked hard to get. Despite his achievement, however, he was troubled by self-doubt and anxiety. He began exploring this, one day, at his poetry therapy group.

Jamie came from a family of doctors. An off-the-cuff remark by his mother, from when he was much younger, had stayed with him; 'You haven't got what it takes – unlike your brother, who is so much smarter than you.'

This one comment haunted Jamie from the very start of his career. It began when he dropped out of university – due to his anxiety – to the dismay of his parents. Years later, when he had earned a good job in an industry he loved, his anxiety stayed with him. Jamie's inner critic – his mother's voice – was always there to bring him down, particularly at those times when he needed encouragement. This led to Jamie having frequent bouts of self-doubt and low confidence. It also left him suffering from imposter syndrome*. He felt like a fraud and was waiting, anxiously, to be found out.

In his poetry therapy group, Jamie was able to explore the impact his mother's comment had had on him. Jamie started to focus on what he was saying to himself, during those periods of self-doubt. In a writing exercise, he was surprised when he wrote down his thoughts; 'I am no good', 'What am I doing here?', 'I have no talent', 'I am not as good as the others'. Once he had noticed these thoughts, he was able to start challenging them, by asking himself, 'Where is the evidence for my belief? Is this really true?'

In time, Jamie was able to 'catch' himself, as soon as he began thinking in this negative way; in doing so, he could, instead, be much kinder to himself. He re-alised that he often felt low after speaking to his mother, so he made sure that he planned a feel-good activity to boost his mood, following these conversations. Jamie finally realised he could not please his parents and decided that he would not allow them to control his life anymore.

Jamie had discovered that, by noticing and challenging his inner critic, he was able to get his anxiety under control.

In my writing for health and wellbeing groups within schools, I explore the importance of working with the inner critic, in order to reduce, or even eliminate, negative self-talk. The poem that follows is by Ella, a Year 9 student from Richmond Park Academy. It has been written in response to the sentence stem, 'As I begin to love myself…'.

In her poem, Ella goes through a process of focusing on the positive and appreciating all aspects of herself, including her flaws.

How to begin
As I begin to love myself
I only concentrate on positive things

As I begin to love myself
I accept my flaws and appreciate my good features

As I begin to love myself
I begin to love more and hate less

As I begin to love myself
I become happy!

Ella
Year 9 Student, Richmond Park Academy

By writing down our thoughts and choosing to become more self-accepting in this way, we can take positive steps towards building resilience and remaining hopeful and optimistic.

The impact of criticism
So far, we have explored the ways in which the inner critic operates in your life. We have also begun to look at the role of external critics. Now it is time to name those external critics and examine their impact.

- Who are your external critics? Think about the people in your life whom you feel have criticised you, in the past, or continue to do so today. Write a list of those individuals.

In her poem, *Marks*, which we explored earlier, Linda Pastan relates the experience of being 'graded' by family members. Grading systems depict a performance at a specific level. They usually involve marks, indicated by numbers or letters, or a pass, fail or merit – which all highlight different levels of attainment.

- What grading systems do your critics use? How do you feel about this criticism?

- What effect does this criticism have on you – in particular on your confidence and resilience? Write down your thoughts.

Remembering unspoken messages

Unspoken messages are messages that are communicated non-verbally, rather than being vocalised. They are sometimes delivered in subtle ways, such as through facial expressions – a raised eyebrow, for example. These messages can be communicated through body language, through tone of voice or through what is not said during a conversation. Let's see, in the next exercise, if you can uncover some unspoken messages. Recognising such messages will help you to understand your inner critic's origin and purpose.

The following exercise is reproduced, with permission, from Lynda Field's *The Self-Esteem Coach: 10 Days to a Confident New You* (Watkins, 2012). Here, the emphasis is on messages from childhood.

Unspoken messages exercise by Lynda Field

What did you learn from the unspoken messages of your childhood? You might have to think deeply before you can complete this exercise; the messages may have been subtle, but the implications will be profound.

Example

The unspoken message was:
'My father ignored me whenever I disagreed with him.'

What I learned from this was:
'If I always pretended to agree with my father he would give me attention.'

The implications of this are:
'I am now often unable to speak my mind and this makes me very angry.'

See if you can recognise an unspoken message from your own past.

- The unspoken message was:

- What I learned from this was:

- The implications of this are:

How did you get on with the exercise from Lynda Field? Consider the question that follows, before you take a break.

- How can you use what you have learned from Lynda Field's exercise, to enhance your confidence and increase your resilience? List three strategies.

Breathing Space

Stop and relax. Feel your feet on the ground and follow your breath, in and out, a few times. Take a moment for yourself.

Naming the inner critic

Let us continue to examine your inner critic. This time, we will focus on giving it an identity. In the activity that follows, you will be invited to choose a metaphor that suits your inner critic. Your metaphor will provide you with a name for the critic and help you uncover its characteristics. This process of naming and describing is important, as it will make it easier for you to work collaboratively with your critic in the future.

In the example on the next page, Mary Geraghty sees her inner critic as a monkey. Later in this chapter, Clare and Emma Afia both see their inner critics as snakes. Helen, meanwhile, sees hers as a crocodile. You might like to use these examples as inspiration for your own writing, in the exercise that follows.

Monkey

If my inner critic were an animal it would be a monkey, a playful character entertaining an audience, showing to the world how harmless it is; little do they know the reality!

Mary Geraghty

- If your inner critic was an animal, what would it be and why? Be sure to pay attention to the details. Think about what your animal eats, as well as when it sleeps, how it moves and what it wants. Is the animal male, female or non-binary? Take note of its habitat, along with where it hides and what time of the day or night it ventures out. Can you hear anything, or is there silence? What can you feel or sense? Include all five senses in your description. Write for ten minutes.

Communicating with your inner critic

What did the last exercise reveal to you? Did you uncover anything, by paying attention to your inner critic's life in the form of an animal? We are going to continue working with the animal metaphor, now, as you complete another writing activity. The exercise that follows is designed to help you understand more about your inner critic's presence – and how it operates.

Communication is an integral part of any relationship. In order to understand your partner, friends, colleagues or family members, you need to communicate effectively with them. This might mean asking questions and clarifying details, rather than mind-reading* – which is a common cognitive distortion, or 'thinking error'. It is crucial to address specific issues when having a potentially difficult conversation. What is not helpful is to blame or attack the other person. This only encourages them to defend and justify their position. In my experience, being aggressive does not usually resolve a situation effectively. It is important, instead, to own your feelings. What is particularly helpful is to say something such as, 'When you act in this way, I feel frustrated/sad/annoyed…' rather than, 'You make me feel…'.

Communicating with the inner critic is no different. It is important to ask questions, to be specific and to avoid being side-tracked by blame or anger.

If you could ask your 'inner critic animal' a question, what would it be? Here is an example from Clare, who posed a set of questions, in the form of a letter:

Dear Rattler,

My memory isn't always great; can you remind me how we met? Where do you come from? Why do you stay here? Do you like being here? Do you like being a rattlesnake?

How long can you stay asleep? *Do* you sleep? What feeds you? Do you belong to me, or are you free to go? Or can I go?
How do you feel about me and the time we've spent together? Do you want to be liked? Do you want to be feared? How long can you live? Do you have any friends? What do you need?

I'm not sure I want you around. I don't think you serve me or help me. I'd like to move away from you, or ask you to leave. Would it be a problem if I did that? Is there something beneficial, that would, then, be missing?

Where do you come from? Do you feed off me - taking away my energy, my life force, for your own? Or are you basically harmless, once I figure you out?
If I admitted I was angry at you, or hated you, would you really go on the attack?

Clare

Now it is your turn. The aim is to gain a better understanding of your inner critic's origin and purpose. You may wish to use some of the questions that Clare poses in her letter. Or you might have your own questions you would like to ask.

- For the time being, list **three** questions.

Letter to your inner critic

In a moment, you will compose a hand-written letter to your inner critic. This type of writing can be useful in relationships – particularly when you feel that your needs are not being met and you want more open communication. A letter can help you to articulate your thoughts and feelings, and to get your point across in a clear and orderly manner. This can then help to form the basis of a constructive dialogue.

- Write a letter to your inner critic. Ask questions to uncover the critic's origin and purpose. Share your own thoughts and feelings, in turn. What particular questions might you ask?

You could include some of the questions from the previous exercise, but may also find that other questions emerge, as you begin to write.

- Do include an address in your letter, plus greetings and salutations. Decide whether you want to write formally or informally to your inner critic, for example, 'Dear…', 'Yours sincerely' – and so on.

- What do you notice about your letter? Did you uncover anything surprising or interesting? Write it down.

We are now going to look at how your inner critic might respond, after receiving your letter.

First, read the two letters by Helen, which were written during a therapeutic writing workshop, entitled 'Write Off Your Inner Critic'. The first is a letter from Helen to her inner critic. The second is the inner critic's response.

Helen's letter to her inner critic:

Dear Mister Crocodile,

I've known of your existence for a while now, so you could say I've got used to how you feature in my life, but my question to you is, 'When will you be satisfied with me?' This is such a big question and I never hear from you when you are satisfied with me; only when you're not. I get the message from you that you want me to move forward with life's events. It feels ok to try out new things, but why do you wait for me to trip up, or for something to not work out? Why can't you be supportive and help me find peace, or resolutions? I am here listening to you, so why can't you listen to me; offer me some help – maybe that could be a break from you?

Helen

Reply from Helen's inner critic:

Dear Helen,

Ok, so I received your letter and – forgive me if I'm wrong, but – you appear to be confused by my presence. I'm here to protect you; keep you safe, stop you from making mistakes. I've seen your past, so I get what you do, and I don't want you to trip up. I know you said that I wait for you to trip up – but I'm just reminding you again, so you can learn from me. You say I'm not supportive and I find that quite dismissive, because I'm always with you. So, my question to you is about how you will be without me, with no-one there to tell you to do it differently, or reminding you of your actual worth. Do you think life will be peaceful without me? I know you very well. Do you think there is more to learn about you that I can't already tell you? You have me down as a bad crocodile. I'm not against you, can you not see this?

Mr Crocodile

- Now it is your turn. Write a reply to your own letter that you wrote to your inner critic, as if your inner critic were speaking to you in return. Try starting with 'Dear [insert your name]…', as Helen did, in the example.

- What did you uncover and learn about your inner critic, from this exercise?

Remember, your inner critic has no authority over you – unless you give it permission to!

B r e a t h i n g   S p a c e

Pause to appreciate your hard work. Allow yourself to take a deep breath, have a yawn and stretch your limbs.

Working constructively with the inner critic

By now, you may have realised that there are several ways of looking at your inner critic. You can see it as an enemy to be overcome, or can think of it as a helpful ally whose function is to support and protect you – albeit in a distorted and somewhat dysfunctional manner.

If we work on the premise that your inner critic is trying to help you, then what, exactly, do you think it is trying to achieve? Perhaps your inner critic is attempting to prevent you from the humiliation of embarrassing yourself? For example, do you need to look over a presentation again, or do one more edit, before an essay is submitted – or perhaps go over your lines before an audition?

Once you recognise when your inner critic has taken the reins in your thoughts – and understand its rationale for doing so – you can then utilise it as an ally and stay in control.

Using an acrostic to engage positively with your inner critic

Here is an example of an acrostic that I wrote a few years ago, which helps me to stay alert to the voice of my inner critic:

I will work with my inner critic: lion,
Never assume it will disappear,
Never assume it can't be tamed.
Ever present,
Roaring, distracting me from being

Courageous, amazing and confident.
Regret fills those times when
I have succumbed and allowed it to
Taint my experiences.
I
Can do this.

- It is your turn, now, to create an acrostic, using the phrase 'inner critic'. Write your first thoughts, without analysing or censoring any of your words. You may wish to write one word – or several words – per line.

I…
N…
N…
E…
R…

C…
R…
I…
T…
I…
C…

Now that you have finished working through this chapter, review the writing you have done and complete the following sentence stem:

- The main insight I gained from this chapter…

Take a moment, now, to acknowledge all your hard work.

Finally, if you would like a reminder - at any point - about how the inner critic can slip in unseen, you may wish to refer to Emma's poem, below.

Snake

Sly and sneaky as it moves
around my body slowly going
from ear to ear whispering

When I hear it moving I
can't speak as it winds its
self around my windpipe so all
I can do is listen

It slithers around the whole
of my body from head to toe
When I do get a chance to open my mouth
instead of me answering it's the
snake.

Emma Afia

To sum up...

- Your inner critic is the voice that sows seeds of doubt.

- Unspoken messages from your childhood can be detrimental in developing confidence and resilience.

- It is your responsibility to silence or turn down the volume of the inner critic.

In the next chapter, we will explore your cherished dreams. We will concentrate, especially, on setting goals that honour your values and your aspirations.

Chapter 5

Awakening the dream

There is no greater agony than bearing an untold story inside you.
Maya Angelou

What happens to a dream deferred?

Our cherished dreams are aspirations that can seem impossible, initially. We can, however, achieve what we desire, so long as we are prepared to act and have the following in place:

- a clear aim

- a realistic action plan

- the right motivation

Have you ever wondered what happens when we defer our dreams? What is the result, when we postpone them or keep putting them off? There are a number of reasons these choices might happen. When dealing with life's adversities, our energy and focus is often geared towards coping with the extra demands placed on us. Your dreams for the future are unlikely to be a priority, for example, when first coming to terms with the death of a loved one, or a job loss. Even when life is going well, you might find yourself suffering from a lack of motivation, or self-belief, which then causes you to procrastinate.

Whatever the case, you can take control of your life and enhance your resilience by revisiting – and accomplishing – your goals. The most difficult experiences can sometimes be the biggest catalysts, to kick-start us into achieving our goals. Can you recall Jenny's experience of recovering from breast cancer in Chapter 3? She was pushed to re-evaluate her priorities, and became determined to make meaningful changes to her life.

What exactly are goals, though? A goal is – quite simply – a dream with a calendar date attached to it. Crucially, however, you must be prepared to put in the work to achieve the goal.

Taking action is a huge part of successful goal-setting. No matter how detailed or compelling your plan may be, if you do not take action it will remain just that – a plan. In his poem, *Harlem*, Langston Hughes – an award winning African American poet, social activist, novelist and playwright, who was a significant figure in the Harlem Renaissance – asks, 'What happens to a dream deferred?'

Harlem

What happens to a dream deferred?

Does it dry up
like a raisin in the sun?
Or fester like a sore—
And then run?
Does it stink like rotten meat?
Or crust and sugar over—
like a syrupy sweet?

Maybe it just sags
like a heavy load.

Or does it explode?

Langston Hughes
*From **The Collected Poems of Langston Hughes,** 1994, published by Alfred A Knopf Inc, © The Estate of Langston Hughes. Reprinted by permission of David Higham Associates.*

Writing in response to a poem

Now is your chance to respond to Hughes's poem. Read the poem again, slowly – and, if possible, aloud – to feel the words in your mouth and get a sense of its rhythms and beats. Pay attention to any emotions or memories it stirs in you. As you complete the sentence stems that follow, imagine that you are speaking to a trusted friend.

- Complete the following sentence stems:

I deferred a dream to… [insert dream] because…

A dream that dried up, like a raisin in the sun, or sagged like a heavy load…

- Read over what you have written and complete the following sentence stem:

  I notice…

- Now change your focus to reflect on a dream that you managed to achieve. Complete the following sentence stem:

I achieved a dream to… [insert dream] because…

- Read over what you have written and complete the following sentence stem: I am aware…

- Consider the difference between the processes of thinking about your deferred dream and thinking about your realised dream. Were there any surprises, or interesting insights? Write for ten minutes.

- What have you learned from this exercise that can help you in the future?

Breathing Space

Stand up and place your feet firmly on the ground. Breathe in deeply, then breathe out again. Turn to your left, then to your right; turn back to the centre and, now, smile as widely as you can.

The power of goals

In the previous exercise, you wrote about the fate of your past dreams and aspirations. Look back over your response to the dream you *did* manage to achieve. How did you feel when writing about it? Did it inspire you? Talking and writing about a dream you have achieved - whether it is summoning up the courage to ask someone out on a date, or reaching the top of Mount Everest - can act as a useful reminder that you can, indeed, succeed. If you struggled to write about a dream that has come true, do return to the prompt at a later date. Perhaps you could write about leaving your home, when you were in a low mood, or about passing a driving test – or the first time you rode a bike.

It is important to set realistic goals, to ensure that your dreams are not pushed further and further away. Goal setting is arguably the most valuable skill you can learn, to improve your confidence and build resilience. It is a powerful tool that focuses your attention on what you want, and allows you to shape your dreams and turn them into reality. Do bear in mind that you may need to take risks and step out of your comfort zone, in order to witness these kinds of exciting changes.

In my experience, not many people write down goals, or a life plan. The very act of writing down your goals engraves them into your subconscious, however. It makes them part of your reality – something tangible that you can see or touch. Your subconscious mind will then work towards achieving the goals that you have set. This same principle applies to capturing goals using drawings, cuttings, collages or a 'vision board'. You will learn more about vision boards later in this chapter.

David Lawrence Preston, in his book *365 Steps to Self-Confidence* (How To Books, 2001), gives this description of the subconscious:

'The mind is often compared to an iceberg, with more than 90% floating below the surface. This hidden mass is the subconscious, a vast storehouse of thoughts, memories and ideas. The subconscious is always listening, watching, soaking up your experiences like a sponge. It then acts as a kind of database to which you constantly refer for guidance and support. Once your subconscious has accepted the idea that you are confident, it makes sure your thinking, feelings and behaviour are brought into line; *it makes confidence your reality.* You can talk to your subconscious, but it responds even better to mental images and emotions.'

We will look, later, at capturing goals in our imagination and harnessing the power of the subconscious, in using vision boards.

Begin with the end in mind

To get started on the journey towards achieving your dreams, we are going to explore how to set successful goals. Where should you begin? In his book *The 7 Habits of Highly Effective People* (Simon & Schuster, 2012), Steven Covey advises us to 'Begin with the end in mind'. He explains that:

'To begin with the end in mind means to start with a clear understanding of your destination. It means to know where you're going, so that you better understand where you are now and so that the steps you take are always in the right direction.'

We are about to visualise 'the end in mind'. Before we do this, take a look at Colin's poem, below, which highlights the importance of self-belief.

What I Want

What I want
Is to not want no more
To be in a place of happiness and tranquil thought
To be at peace in my mind and not constantly at war
With me, myself and I
So I can break free to soar
I need to start to believe in thee
- thee being me -
Before I can achieve and see
The stones that create the path
And trust in where it's leading me
To throw myself in 100% to every opportunity
So I can be what I want
And get to where I need to be

Colin

Resident, Her Majesty's Prison Risley
Inspired by Linda Pastan's poem, **What We Want**

How did you respond to Colin's poem? Perhaps his lack of self-belief resonated with you or maybe his poem offered you the motivation you need to start along your own path towards your dreams.

Now, it is time to get a clearer picture of what those dreams look like. The following visualisation is designed to help you decide on the direction you want your life to take - so, it might be a good idea to 'dream big'! Read the visualisation text through - at least twice - before getting started. You could, perhaps, ask someone to read it to you, as another method of familiarising yourself with the content; alternatively, you might record the visualisation (e.g., using the 'voice' function on a smartphone). When you reach the stage of then performing your visualisation, you might find it helpful to keep your eyes closed throughout the process. If you feel uncomfortable at any time, though, or if the visualisation is not working for you, open your eyes.

Visualisation: Future celebration

Find a comfortable place. Take a minute to relax. This might include putting any smartphone aside, kicking off your shoes and getting more comfortable. Now, take some deep breaths. Close your eyes for a moment and give yourself permission to let your imagination run free, about your future.

When you are ready, bring an image of yourself into your mind's eye. Imagine a future point in your life, which involves a celebration dedicated entirely to you. It could be your retirement party, a birthday party or any other significant milestone – at whatever age you choose. At this celebration, your life is exactly the way you want it to be. You are happy, healthy, motivated and stress-free. You are having an amazing time at your event, as you have been living the life that you desired. Will you be married, or settled down with a family, or will you be single? What about your friends, family members and colleagues? Who will be there?

You are having a great time! Your favourite music is playing in the background – and you are elated that you have become the person you wanted to be. Imagine all the incredible things you have done – and are still doing. Think about the person you are, at that point – and about all the things you have managed to accumulate in your life that are important to you.

Imagine all the lives you have touched and the differences you have made. What type of legacy will you leave? Hold on to that image. Allow the image to become vivid and bold.

If you had children, did you enjoy raising your family? Did you love supporting your loved ones? What about voluntary work? If you chose to work, what about your career? Did you become a valued member of your company? Did you become your own boss?

Imagine the flat, house, cottage, mansion or other dwelling you are living in, at that point. Who are your neighbours? Where will you go on your next holiday? Let's just spend a few moments picturing this scene. How do you get around town, or the seaside or countryside? Is it in a car? If so, what make and model is it? What about the colour? Or do you cycle? Or own a motorbike you had always dreamed of?

As you say, 'Thank you', to all those who have been part of your journey, reflect on the things you will be doing in the future. Who will you be spending more time with? What types of activities will make you happy, since you have been given - or created - more free time? What about the new skills you will acquire, or hobbies you will start, or continue to do?

Take a few moments. Breathe in the atmosphere from your celebration. Stay with this feeling for a while.

When you are ready, open your eyes and come back to the comfortable place you began from. Move your neck, gently, from side to side. Stretch out your arms. Then, take a few breaths, as you allow your mind to become more alert.

You have just visualised your goals! You may well have a clearer picture of how you want your life to be, in the future, or going forward. It is now time to record the details in writing.

- When you are ready, write down all the nourishing and fulfilling things that you saw in your visualisation. Reflect, in your writing, on the person you had become. Write as though this is all happening now, however, using the first person and present tense (i.e.,' I am...'). Reflect, also, on the skills and possessions you managed to accumulate that were especially important to you. Include as much detail as possible. It may take several pages to describe the life you are living in your visualisation. Take as long as you need, before continuing with the rest of this exercise.

- Read over what you have written and complete the following sentence stem:

Now I have read what I have written, I notice/feel…

Breathing Space

Take a well-earned break, before moving on to the next section. Allow yourself to take a deep breath, have a yawn and stretch your limbs.

You cannot eat an elephant whole

Let's continue with the process of setting successful goals. Using information from your visualisation, you are about to complete a step-by-step process that will solidify your goals and help you create a clear action plan. As part of this, you will write goals down in the form of affirmations. You will also check your goals against the values that you identified in Chapter 3. Finally, you will explore the actions you can take in order to move forward with your dream.

Before we start, read the following story about how Aaliyah achieved her goal of securing a dream job.

Aaliyah was a stay-at-home mum, in her mid-forties, who lived in an affluent neighbourhood in West London. She attended the coaching programme, 'Relaunch Your Career', shortly after her divorce.

Aaliyah had given up her career in design when her daughter was born. From then, onwards, she dedicated her life to raising her children and supporting her husband in his work as a highly respected engineer. When Aaliyah attended her first coaching session, she lacked confidence. She was still emotional, at times, about the breakup of her family – and felt even less positive about her career.

Aaliyah believed that her lack of recent work experience – and the fact that she hadn't attended a job interview in over ten years – would prevent her from being employed. This limiting belief was quickly challenged. First, Aaliyah needed to be clear about exactly what type of job she wanted – and why she wanted it.

When talking about her motivations, she expressed how she was keen to change her legacy. Aaliyah felt it was important for her daughters to be more independent and she also wanted to be an inspiration to them. As well as this, she wanted a career that she would love doing – one that would allow her to be creative and give freedom to try out her own ideas. She wanted to make decisions and plan her work with little supervision.

Through the coaching programme, Aaliyah focused on identifying those transferrable skills that she used already, in successfully running her home. Aaliyah's role as a mother involved similar skills to those required in the workplace, such as health and safety, planning, prioritising, training and financial management – as well as taking the initiative when dealing with challenges.

Once Aaliyah was able to recognise her experience and skill set, she felt more confident about applying for jobs. Three months after the coaching programme ended, Aaliyah found a job that was exactly right for her – as an interior designer at a prestigious company. She was incredibly pleased with the role, which included flexible working hours so that she could maintain a happy and balanced lifestyle.

In the story above, Aaliyah focused on just one goal – obtaining a job she enjoyed – and she achieved it. Whatever aspirations you have for your own life, it is important that you do not try to work on too many goals at once, since this could overwhelm you, quickly. Keep in mind that you cannot eat an elephant whole; you can only do it one bite at a time!

I suggest that you take each of your goals in turn and go through the 'Action Planning for Success' process, below, for each one, individually. For example, you might choose to focus on a new car, initially, then on a new home; and then a change of career, followed by improved health – and so on.

If you are not sure which goal to choose first, start with the easiest or quickest. This will boost your confidence and motivate you to achieve your other goals.

Action Planning for Success

What follows is a step-by-step guide to setting your goals, presented in actionable sections. You will cover five key areas:

- Your goal

- Your motivation

- Your actions

- Barriers

- Moving forward

This is your chance to create an action plan for success. Take your time, as you consider each of your goals in detail, alongside the underlying principles of successful goal setting. Go through the full process for each goal. You may need to revisit this exercise from time to time, as you work through your goals in a systematic way.

Your goal

- **Your goal needs to be specific.** Choose the first goal you want to focus on and write it down, in one sentence. Try to be as succinct as possible. Read your goal out loud. Does it sound and feel right? If not, remain patient, as you may need to write the sentence out a few times until it sounds and feels right to you.

- **Your goal needs to be framed in the positive.** The subconscious accepts whatever you put into it, and moves towards achievement. Write in the present tense and describe exactly what you want – rather than what you do not want – or, indeed, what you think you *should* want. For example,, 'I am healthy', rather than, 'I will give up smoking'. Read your goal out loud. Do you feel emotionally connected to this goal? If not, try writing it out a few more times, until you find words that sound and feel right to you.

- **Your goal needs to be realistic.** When you set an unrealistic goal, you set yourself up for disappointment. For example, you cannot expect to set a goal to take part in a marathon if the marathon is only three weeks away!

- **Your goal needs to be measurable and given a time frame.** How will you know that you have achieved this goal? Write it down. Be specific. For example, 'I will know when I am dress size 12, in six months' time' or 'I will know when I have completed three chapters of my book, by the end of May'.

Your motivation

- **Your goal must be important to you and in line with your values.** If you are emotionally connected to the goal and feel inspired by it, this will help you stay motivated when times get tough. Reflect on the values list that you created near the beginning of Chapter 3. Now, ask yourself, 'Why is this goal important to me?' Write for seven minutes.

Your actions

- Think carefully about the following question: What have you already tried, in order to improve your situation or achieve your goal?

- What *could* you do now that is within your control and will move you one step closer to your goal? Write down five actions.

- If you went to a friend, partner or manager for advice about this goal, what might they suggest? Make a long list.

- Read your goal out loud. Commit it to the Universe.

Barriers

- What obstacles or barriers prevent, or hinder, you from moving towards your goal?

- How can you overcome these obstacles or barriers?

- How will you remain motivated?

- Who else can help you with this goal – and how?

Moving forward

- Looking over the answers you noted down in the "Your actions" section, choose the first action that you will take forward. Write it down.

- When will you take this action? What is a realistic timescale? Write down the date and time.

- Choose a confident or optimistic person, who will hold you accountable for achieving this goal. Decide when you are going to call - or send a message to - this person, explaining what you are aiming to achieve and asking for their help. Write down the date and time.

You have now set your goal, successfully and decided on a specific next step to take. Next, complete that step and continue taking further actions, until you achieve the goal.

When you are ready, you can go through this process again, with another goal. Bear in mind that you may need to revisit and review your plans periodically and make changes where necessary, as your priorities and situations change. This is a natural part of the process.

Finally, consider how you will celebrate and reward yourself, when you complete your chosen actions and reach your goals. You deserve to enjoy your success!

Breathing Space

Stop and relax for a moment. Feel your feet on the ground and the chair supporting your body. Follow your breath; observe it moving in and out. Do this a couple of times and then stretch.

Three simple questions

So far, we have looked at what happens when your dreams are deferred. We have also detailed your dreams and goals as they stand, and gone through a process of action planning to help give you the best chances of success. Before you act on each of your goals, you might like to try the following, additional exercise.

Firstly, write down your chosen goal and read it out loud. Secondly, as you think about achieving your goal, ask yourself these three simple questions and note down your responses:

- What is the worst thing that could happen?

- What is the best thing that could happen?

- What is the most likely thing that could happen?

Take some time to reflect on the writing you have just completed, before responding to the following question:

- What else do I need to consider? Again, write down your answer.

Keeping your dreams alive

In a moment, we will go through an exercise that will help you to stay focused on the tasks ahead and keep your dreams alive. First, however, we will explore the main tool of the exercise – which is the vision board.

A vision board is a visual representation of your goals and dreams. When coupled with an action plan, it can be an effective way to work with the 'law of attraction' – that is, to attract into your life anything that you focus on and help make your vision a reality.

In the story that follows, you will see how Lisa used a vision board as part of her goal – to find a permanent home.

> *Lisa was an introverted, single mum, in her forties, who first learned about vision boards at a 'Setting Goals for Success' workshop. At the beginning of the session,*

Lisa and the rest of the group were taken through the process of identifying their goals and creating action plans. Then they were invited to put their imaginations to work. As Lisa had never created a vision board before, the coach suggested she start with one that encompassed all of her goals.

Lisa set to work finding pictures and photos that depicted good health, wealth and her family. She also included an image of a Georgian house. She yearned for a place that she could truly called home. Lisa's home situation was precarious. She had moved several times – in recent years – and was trying hard to maintain stability for herself and two teenage sons.

Lisa thoroughly enjoyed the opportunity to use her imagination and work simultaneously on her goals. Being creative helped to unleash new ideas, as well as boosting her mood. She felt even more energised, as she discussed her vision board and listened to other participants in the group. Her goals felt much more achievable.

Walking down her local high street, a few years later, Lisa bumped into the coach from her workshop. She explained, excitedly, that she never gave up her dream of being in a place that she could call home – and was now living in a Georgian house! She attributed this achievement to following through on her plan, and having her vision board in a place where she could see it daily.

If, like Lisa, you have never created a vision board before, I would suggest starting with one that includes all of your goals – rather than creating separate boards for individual aims or areas of life. You may wish to use the goals you identified from your visualisation earlier in this chapter; but it is entirely up to you.

You can opt to create a traditional vision board (as shown overleaf), as Lisa did, or use an online version. An online vision board is quick and easy to do, and can be accessed on a phone or computer, at any point. Vision board apps can be downloaded online for free. Several apps have built-in images, but you can also use your own photos, add music and gain inspiration from other users. Once your vision board is complete, you might decide to use it as the wallpaper background, on your computer or phone.

There are no rules when creating a vision board, other than making sure you depict what you really want out of life – as opposed to what society dictates, or what others think you should want.

Creating a traditional vision board

This involves a more practical approach, which will require art materials, such as: a large piece of cardboard or paper, scissors, glue, Blu Tack – and plenty of magazines and newspapers.

We will focus on setting the date, first and then prepare to set the mood. Finally, we will delve into the detail, by creating the vision board contents.

Set the date: First, identify a date in your diary when you can create your vision board. This is one of the most important activities you will ever do, so give yourself plenty of time; creating your vision board should not be rushed. Many people create vision boards at the start of a new year, or after a significant transition in life.

Set the mood: Now that you are ready to proceed with creating the vision board, find yourself a pleasant space and switch off any visual technology distractions, such as your TV, computer or smartphone.

You may want to create your vision board in silence, or, alternatively, play relaxing music in the background. You could, additionally, light a candle. Focus your attention on the here and now; take a few long, deep breaths, and consider all the things you are grateful for in your life.

Start creating: Take a large piece of cardboard or flipchart-sized piece of paper, along with scissors, glue and plenty of magazines and newspapers. You may need to tape pieces of flipchart paper together, so that you can include all of your dreams. Once you start, you will likely be surprised by how quickly you can fill up your paper or board! Follow these guidelines, to make the most of your vision board:

- Make sure you have a selection of images and words, from a range of sources that resonate or inspire you. Choose a good variety of magazines and newspapers. You can go online to search for pictures, images or symbols that represent your dreams, along with quotes, sayings and inspiring slogans. Include high-quality photos, postcards, drawings and poems (written by yourself or others), to represent your goals.

- It is crucial that you consider the details of what you want in your overall image, as whatever you illustrate on your vision board will likely become your reality! (Remember Lisa's success, as mentioned earlier in the chapter).

- Cut out the images and – before you glue them on your piece of cardboard or paper – lay everything out, so you gain a good idea of where you want each element to go. Move things around, until it all feels right. Putting things in the right place is important. Make sure that what you create feels right for you, instinctively.

- To make your vision board even more compelling, put yourself in the picture; add a drawing or photograph of yourself achieving your goals.

- Remember to include positive affirmations (we looked at creating these near the end of Chapter 3). Phrases, such as, 'I love driving my new white Range Rover', or, 'I enjoy spending plenty of quality time with my friends and family' will help reinforce your aspirations.

- Also consider adding inspirational quotes or images that remind you of how you will feel, once your dreams are achieved.

Your vision board is ready to go! By touching and looking at it daily, you will have a clear vision for your life and feel inspired to create the future you deserve. Remember to put it in a place where you can see it every day.

Now that you have finished working through this chapter, review the writing you have done and complete the following sentence stem:

- The main insight I gained from this chapter...

Take a moment, now, to acknowledge all your hard work.

Finally, if you would like a reminder, at any point, about how poetry can be used to consider your dreams, you may wish to refer to Sparrow's poem, below.

Some Folks

Some folks find it really easy to speak their minds
Words roll off their tongues so eloquently
They are storytellers of their own lives
But I don't
I can't
I won't

My story comes out on pages
Always ending up in rhythm or rhyme
I want to feel the freedom from anxiety

To know what it's like to stand tall & confident
So I too can SPEAK my mind
And experience the enjoyment of living all the dreams which I have inside.

Sparrow

To sum up...

- Having realistic goals, to work towards, helps you take control and build your resilience.

- Your goal will remain a dream, unless you combine it with action-planning.

- Vision boards are some of the most effective ways to stay focused and keep your dreams alive.

In the next chapter, we will concentrate on how you can let go of any emotions and past experiences that may keep you stuck, so that you can move towards a more fulfilling future.

Chapter 6

Learning to let go

To let go is not to regret the past, but to grow and live for the future.
Anonymous

Learning lessons from our scars

In Lemn Sissay's memoir, *My Name Is Why*, the BAFTA-nominated award-winning writer and broadcaster says, 'I am not defined by scars but by the incredible ability to heal.'

Most of us, at some point in our lives, have yearned to be set free from a negative experience. In this chapter we will look at how to 'let go' of some aspects of the past – so they do not control our future – thereby allowing us to heal. First, we need to explore the various types of emotional wounds that we accumulate, along with the scars we must tend to, as a result. The type of wound will determine both the treatment and length of the healing process.

All of us have experienced healing in a physical sense. We know that a flesh wound can heal well on its own. A deep gash may take a bit longer and could require someone to examine and dress it carefully. The more severe the wound, the greater the likelihood that medical or professional help will be needed. A physical scar is a mark left on the skin, or within body tissue, where a wound, burn or sore has not healed completely and fresh tissue has developed. That area of the skin is never the same again. It may be tender to the touch and irritate you, from time to time. If it is unsightly, you may attempt to disguise it, covering it with clothes, hair (if the scar is on, or near, the face) or make-up. Nevertheless, you still know it is there. It remains a reminder of the original injury.

We also have emotional scars, where we have experienced the heart-breaking disappointments of mistreatment, rejection, betrayal or abandonment. These scars are not usually visible to the naked eye, but can show up in our behaviours. What we do with these emotional scars, and the way we wear them, is of vital importance. Do you wear your scar like a badge of honour, or do you cover it up? To 'let go', in this context, is to witness the scar, open up the wound, tentatively, and acknowledge the pearls of wisdom to be gained, whilst accepting the lessons that life has taught you. Maybe a scar worn as a badge of honour tells you that you need people to recognise both your pain and your strength. Perhaps a scar that has been covered up is a sign that you feel shame over what happened in the past – and about what you did, or did not do. Whatever you have been through, now is the time to reach towards compassion for yourself and accept your feelings as a sign of your humanity. When we accept ourselves – warts and all – our self-compassion helps to strengthen our resilience.

Whilst difficulties are usually unpleasant, they can be mixed blessings. In time and with the right support, you may be able to see a 'silver lining', whilst also acknowledging and working through any sad, or otherwise painful feelings.

In my case, even though I did not know it at the time, some difficult and traumatic experiences I went through in my late teens and early twenties set me on the path towards helping others. I am grateful for my friends, who were – and still remain – an invaluable source of support. They are part of my silver lining, together with the fulfilling career I have today.

It is worth recognising, of course, that in some circumstances there is no silver lining or benefit. In those situations, self-compassion is even more vital.

To let go of the past takes enormous courage. We cannot necessarily forget that past, although we may often be encouraged to – and would perhaps like to do so. It is a part of our personal history and will be with us always. We can, however, accept life lessons from the past and prevent it from limiting or imprisoning us. To do this, it is essential that we acknowledge our scars and name our losses, so we can grieve and find healing.

Grieving the old story

A few years ago, I was fortunate to attend a workshop by US author and grief educator, Ted Bowman, entitled "Exploring Resilience with Ted Bowman Using Writing, Poetry and Stories". In the workshop, Bowman talked about the loss of dreams. He described how we create pictures in our minds of personal worlds and form strong, emotional attachments to these images. Such pictures communicate powerful messages to us, about the way we imagine life is supposed to be. Being forced to let go of these images is part of the 'loss of dreams'. Examples of this loss could include a relationship break-up, which has meant that you and your partner will never grow old together. Or you may have experienced the loss of a baby at birth, and part of your bereavement is never being able to experience the school run with that child. You may, alternatively, have a mental illness or disability, which prevents you from enjoying the life you expected. In essence, your dreams have been shattered and you feel a real sense of life being unfair, since these circumstances rob you of 'what might have been'.

In his booklet on the subject, entitled *Loss of Dreams: A Special Kind of Grief* (Ted Bowman, 1994), Bowman emphasises the importance of naming the loss and letting go of the old pictures of how we expect our life will be. We need to make room for new images of ourselves and the world, and open the way for our next story. Sometimes – when it seems a loss is too much for us to bear – we bury the feelings, along with anything else associated with our loss. We may refuse to talk about it. As Bowman frequently says, however, 'If something is unmentionable, it's also unmanageable.'

Before we delve into those lost dreams, we will look at what helped Femi to cope with loss, during a difficult period of her life.

Femi, a 33-year-old teaching assistant, lived with her partner in London. Every Friday, after work, she would buy some popcorn and a bottle of wine and then use the underground to travel to her parents' home, in Middlesex. It was her weekly movie night with her younger brothers, Michael and Emmanuel.

This particular day was just like any other Friday, except that Femi was running late. She didn't have time to buy snacks before catching her train and, by the time she reached her destination, she had completely forgotten about getting the popcorn and wine. She arrived empty-handed at her parents' home.

Michael, her youngest brother, offered to go to the shop, quickly, before the movie started. But he never returned.

Michael had been struck down by a car, which the family later learned was driven by a drunk driver. Femi was devastated. Her feelings swung, uncontrollably, between sadness and anger. Like many people who experience a bereavement, Femi blamed herself. If only she'd remembered the snacks! What if she'd told Michael to stay put and gone to the shop instead of him?

Weighed down by guilt, Femi realised she needed to lean on her partner and her wider support systems. She wasn't afraid to ask for help – when things became too overwhelming – and was specific when communicating what she needed. She asked her best friend, Janet, to check on her regularly in the first few weeks, after Michael's death. Janet always checked how Femi was doing and allowed her to talk about whatever she wanted.

On some days, Femi wanted to talk about her emotions and how sad she was feeling. On other days, she wanted to talk about what was happening with their circle of friends.

Counselling – something Femi would never have considered before – was suggested by another friend, who had recently started seeing a counsellor after a difficult break up. This became a great resource for Femi. Counselling helped her to process her current pain and also uncover other significant losses in her life – such as the death of a much-loved family pet, and the end of her career in the city. These were events that she had not realised were still having an impact on her. She was keen, now, to deal with them and move on.

Femi discovered that, by reaching out to those around her, she found ways to cope with her loss. Through counselling, she also discovered the impact of other, unresolved losses in her life.

In the exercise that follows, you will have a chance to explore your own losses. Take your time with this exercise, particularly if you have experienced many losses during your life. List a few – and, then, come back to this exercise again, when you feel ready.

- What losses do you find unmentionable?

List them.

- Write about your thoughts and feelings associated with each loss.

If you have experienced a number of losses, you may wish to write a small amount about them now and then return to this exercise again later.

- How can you grieve these losses?

- What could be your first step?

- What would be the last step?

- Create a piece of writing that involves you having fun and enjoying life in the future. This could take the form of a poem, a piece of prose, a letter – or any other form of writing that you feel comfortable with. I suggest you give your piece of writing a title, such as: "**New Dreams**" or "**New Story**".

Breathing Space

Stand up and put your feet firmly on the ground. Breathe in deeply and out again. Turn to your left, then to your right turn back to the centre – and, now, smile as widely as you can.

Recognising your scars

How did you get on with the last exercise? What did it feel like, to consider your new dreams? Perhaps you only got as far as naming your losses – in which case, do come back to this exercise again, whenever you feel able to.

In the writing exercises that follow, we will consider the scars that you may be wearing. It is important to understand the impact they can have on your mental, physical and spiritual wellbeing – as well as on other people around you.

- What scars are you wearing? Be gentle, because opening up old wounds can be painful. Try to list the scars, using a minimum number of words – perhaps just one or two, where possible.

Breathing Space

Use **3, 2, 1**: Look around you. Notice three things you can see and two things you can hear. Now take one deep, cleansing breath.

Wearing your scars

The poem entitled, *Into the Hour*, featured in *New Collected Poems* (Carcanet, 2002), by English poet Elizabeth Jennings, inspired me to write the following, five-line poem:

Heaven

I wear the scar of
Betrayal,
So deep oceans dare not undress
Horse-Eye jacks pause and gaze
Yearning for explanation.

As you can see from my example, a poem may be completely personal; it does not have to make sense to anyone else. Poetry has value as a powerful form of expression for the person writing it.

- I would like to encourage you to create your own, simple, five-line poem. Bear in mind that it is not necessary for poems to rhyme. To start you off, I suggest using the following words in your opening line:

'I wear the scar of…'.

- Give your poem a title, once you have finished.

Breathing Space

When you have completed your poem and given it a title, take another deep breath; have a yawn and a stretch.

- What do you notice about your poem? Did you uncover anything surprising or find anything interesting? Write it down.

- What mental, physical and spiritual impact has your scar (or scars) had on you and those closest to you?

- What lessons have you learned from your scars? Write for three minutes, using the following sentence stem as your prompt:

I have learned that…

Acknowledging life lessons

Magdalena, a Year 9 student from Richmond Park Academy, reminds us, in her poem, below, about the importance of hope. She tells us that, no matter how bad things are, life does go on – and it will get better. Perhaps we can learn from Magdalena and remember this, as we deal with our own challenges and develop a strategy for survival.

I've learned that

I've learned that no matter
what happens, or how
bad it seems today,
life does go on, and
it will be better tomorrow

Magdalena
Year 9 Student

As Nicholas found out, in Chapter 2, it sometimes seems impossible to acknowledge the harsh lessons we have learned from our scars – particularly when these lessons come from our own families, or the people closest to us. Yet we must do so – at some point. Once we have processed and explored our feelings and, then, understood the lessons, we can try to let go of any pain that may have been locked up in our experiences. If we do not do so, we will simply keep replaying the past and holding onto the pain.

Each person will have their own process and time span for recognising, working through and understanding their emotions. Beth Jacobs, in her book *Writing for Emotional Balance* (New Harbinger Publications, 2004), says, 'Emotion management is a lifelong, ongoing process; it is not something you perfect or finish.'

If you need help, do consider making an appointment to see a counsellor, or psychotherapist, who can support you with this.

Throwing off your heavy coat

In this section we are going to explore the payoffs that our problems can offer, which can make them particularly difficult to shed. In a moment, I will invite you to write in response to the poem, *Coat*, featured in her collection, ***Close Relatives*** (Secker & Warburg, 1981), by Vicki Feaver – an award-winning poet, living in Scotland. This may help you to find new ways to let go and prevent your issues becoming a part of your identity. Read the poem once; before we go through the writing exercise.

Coat

Sometimes I have wanted
to throw you off
like a heavy coat.

Sometimes I have said
you would not let me
breathe or move.

But now that I am free
to choose light clothes
or none at all

I feel the cold
and all the time I think
how warm it used to be.

Vicki Feaver

Reproduced with permission from Vicki Feaver.

In Feaver's poem, she talks about wanting to throw someone – or something – off, 'like a heavy coat'. Our problems can often feel like the weight of a heavy coat, which we choose to wear continually. Indeed, if a problem has been with us for a long time it can fit seamlessly and start to seem snug. After a while we may not even realise that the problem has become *us*; it has merged with our identity. Our issue is now being 'worn', as part of our personality.

If we are being truly honest, we may not actually want to throw off our heavy coat. As peculiar as it might seem, sad and painful feelings can be extremely familiar and comfortable – something we have been accustomed to, throughout our lives. We may end up feeling naked and vulnerable without them.

This moment might be a good time for some honesty. Ask yourself, 'Do I *really* want to throw off my heavy coat? Do *I* really want to change?' Before you fully answer these questions for yourself, take a look at Peter's situation.

Peter was a quiet, 24-year-old, who lived with his parents and younger sister. His mother, Sophia, spent most of her time in the family home while his father was a pilot, who often flew long-haul.

One day, while attending his 'Writing for Self-Discovery' group, Peter was invited to respond to the poem, 'Coat'. He reluctantly described his mother, Sophia, as his 'heavy coat'.

Peter spoke about how Sophia, aged 53, had suffered a mild stroke five years ago and, as a result, struggled with her mobility at times. Peter soon became the person who ran errands for her. He helped her around the house, did the shopping and accompanied her to medical appointments – even when his father was at home. Sophia was happy to depend heavily on her son and seemed to rely on him for emotional – as well as practical – support. Peter recalled how he would take time off from work, to keep his mother company when she was feeling low. When Peter did go to work, he would often worry about leaving her alone and would feel guilty.

Peter was happy to help his mother at first. Over time, however, it became a burden. He didn't see much of his friends and found it difficult to meet anyone romantically. All of this was hard for Peter to talk about, particularly as he loved his mother and had a good relationship with her.

As time went by, Peter began noticing that his mother often embellished her ailments and made her situation seem much worse than it actually was. He realised that Sophia was enjoying the support and attention she received. Meanwhile, she never seemed to show much interest in Peter's own life or work. This upset him, as he valued his mother's opinion.

Whilst Peter described his mother as his 'heavy coat', it was clear to the writing group that Sophia also had a 'heavy coat' of her own – one that had become her personality. If Sophia were to honestly answer the question, 'Do I really want *to throw off my heavy coat', she probably wouldn't want to change! She would perhaps be aware that, if she did make changes, the world around her would also change. In this circumstance, her ill health – or 'heavy coat' – was serving a purpose. Being stuck meant that her son, Peter, was always there for her. If she became 'unstuck', then perhaps he would stop giving her so much attention? His attention was the <u>payoff</u> she received, for continuing in her role as a person unable to cope by herself.*

Peter's support was the reward Sophia received, by remaining dependent on other people. In situations such as these, it is important to consider the payoff – the reward – and be honest about our own wants and needs.

Let's look more closely at the "payoff" system. If you are repeating a self-destructive, or frustrating, behaviour, then you have invested in that system or habit, because, on some level – usually deep down – there is a reward.

You may not agree with this at first, because it does not seem to make sense. However, consider that, if a negative behaviour did not offer some sort of benefit or reward, you would probably discard it. It is likely that you are carrying out such a behaviour because, on an unconscious level, you receive some kind of payoff for it. Peter was surprised when he completed the following exercise. It offered him valuable insight and helped him make some necessary changes in his relationship with his mother. He began to encourage his mother to do things for herself and rely on her own support systems, as well as seek support from his father. Peter realised that, when he didn't allow his mother to do for herself – even though she was capable – he was denying her an opportunity to develop and grow.

Let us see if this exercise can help you to uncover the reasons that you might adopt a particular behaviour and continue to 'wear' a problem, as if it was a heavy coat.

Writing in response to a poem

Read the poem, 'Coat', slowly – and aloud, so that you can feel the words in your mouth and get a sense of the poem's pulse and beats. Pay attention to any thoughts, emotions or memories it brings up, and imagine what you would say to a close friend, or other confidante, about your reactions to the poem.

- Write about a 'heavy coat' that you successfully threw off. What strategies did you use?

- What issues are you currently dealing with? Do any of them feel like a heavy coat?

- Complete the following sentence stem:

Now that I am free…

- If appropriate, what payoff – or underlying benefit – are you getting from wearing your heavy coat?

- Read over your last piece of writing and complete the following sentence stem:

Now that I have read what I have written, I notice, or am surprised to find….

Breathing Space

Therapeutic writing can leave you feeling exhausted, so do remember to schedule in regular breaks. It may be useful for you to take a break now, before you move on to the next section.

Writing your autobiography

So far, in this chapter, we have explored our lost dreams, looked at the lessons we can learn from our scars and considered the concept of payoffs. A core part of building resilience is to recognise your own personal process for letting go. In order to do this, it can be useful to contemplate the larger story of your life. This will allow you to identify positive patterns from the past and understand more about how you were able to overcome adversity.

In this next exercise, I would like to encourage you to write your autobiography. It need not be as daunting as it sounds! I suggest that you borrow the structure from Portia Nelson's poem, *Autobiography in Five Short Chapters*, which we looked at in Chapter 2.

Follow the steps that follow, to create your own autobiography in five chapters:

- Think over situations in your life that you have successfully overcome. These could be anything from completing an essay to finishing university or dealing with divorce – in fact, in managing any anxiety-provoking situation. Note down the events in chronological order.

- Reflect, in your writing, on the events you have just written down. How did you overcome them? What resources did you draw on to help you? Pay attention to any patterns that emerge. Consider the general way(s) in which you have dealt with challenging and new situations.

- Using your notes from the steps above, write your autobiography in five short chapters. Remember, you can borrow the structure from Portia Nelson's poem 'Autobiography in Five Short Chapters'.

- When you have completed your autobiography, give the piece of writing a title.

Breathing Space

Pause to appreciate your hard work. Allow yourself to take a deep breath, yawn – and stretch your limbs. It may be useful to take a longer break, now, before you move on to the next section.

Working with your unique process

In the previous writing activity, you had the chance to write your autobiography in five chapters and identify some of the important transitions and challenges you have overcome, during your life. Let us now examine the process you went through to deal with those challenges and transitions.

- Revisit your autobiography in five short chapters. Where you notice a transition, or challenge, note it down.

- Reflect, in your writing, on your process for overcoming each transition or challenge. Break it down and note the steps you took to succeed. Can you identify where your process started? Did you begin with your head buried in the sand, or were you aware of what was happening right from the start?

- What helped you to overcome each transition? What did you do, specifically, to take your head out of the sand – or to begin moving forward?

- What did you do next?

- What else did you do?

Write down the steps you took. Aim to list them using three or four words, only.
1...
2...
3...
4...
5...

- Finally, comment on any strong feelings or emotions that occurred just now, as you re-called your life experiences and wrote about them. Write for three minutes.

Unsent letter

Recognising where you are, in your process, can help strengthen your resolve.

Did you manage to work through the last exercise and identify your own unique way(s) of handling difficult situations?

Whilst you may have become more aware of your process, you might have also discovered that you find it hard to let go of strong emotions. Letter writing is a useful way to express your feelings and come to terms with a situation. You may remember that we used letter writing, near the end of Chapter 4, to communicate with your inner critic. We will now look at how 'unsent letters' can help you release strong emotions and move on.

Have you ever written a letter or email and, then, decided to not send it for one reason or another? Did you notice that your state of mind improved, after writing? Unsent letters are dif-ferent from standard letters: you never deliver them to the recipient and therefore do not need to worry about any consequences. The purpose is for *you* – the writer – to vent, release, offload, and seek clarity. You can write an unsent letter to any person or organisation you perceive as having hurt or wronged you, in some way. You could also choose to write an unsent letter to someone who is deceased, to help you deal with any unfinished business.

The subject focus of your letter can, alternatively, be more abstract. For instance, you may want to set yourself free from your feelings around a health issue, in which case you could write an unsent letter to your cancer, or your heart attack.

There is no need to share your letter with anyone else. The important part is writing the letter in the first place.

A word of caution: if you cannot promise yourself that you will never send the letter, then I suggest you do not write it at this point. You are probably not ready to work through the emotions just yet.

People who do feel ready to tackle this exercise may still find it daunting, initially, but it is a powerful way to rid yourself of negative thoughts and overwhelming emotions. Do give yourself permission to be as honest and open as you can. Writing an unsent letter allows you to say the unsayable. It enables you to express your pain, frustration, confusion and shame, in a way that cannot be expressed directly to the recipient. It is also a great opportunity to vent your frustrations and feelings about the wider support – or lack of support – you have received from your partner, colleagues, family or friends, during a difficult time.

Tips for writing an unsent letter

- **When to write:** Choose a time when you will not be interrupted. Give yourself plenty of time and space, to allow for any uncomfortable or unpleasant feelings that may arise.

- **Where to write:** You may wish to write alone – perhaps at home, in your own quiet space, or with music in the background. If you prefer to write in the company of strangers, then the setting of a café or park might suit you better.

- **Plan to dispose of your letter:** Create a ritual. Whatever you do, make sure you decide in advance exactly how you will dispose of your letter – if, indeed, you intend to do that. Will you burn it, shred it, rip it up into tiny pieces, flush it down the toilet or bury it in the garden?

- **What to write:** You may want to write about a typical day in the presence of the person, organisation or illness you are addressing – or about a specific incident that you recall. Write about your feelings. Describe the extent of the hurt you experienced from this person or entity. Explain the reasons you wish to let them go, where relevant.

- **Ask questions:** Ask your recipient questions, such as, 'Why did you do this to me? What do you want from me? Why me? What do you get out of hurting me?'

- **Do something you enjoy:** Before you sit down to write your unsent letter, make sure that you have an event, or activity, planned, to enjoy immediately afterwards.

Now is your chance to write an unsent letter of your own. Use this as an opportunity to release yourself from thoughts and emotions that have been holding you back.

- Choose one of the options that follow. Write an unsent letter to the person or entity who:

  a. You perceive has hurt you the most

  b. You find the hardest to forgive

  c. You believe prevents you from enjoying your life and experiencing inner peace

  d. You are in conflict with.

Bear in mind that the person could be you, in all cases!

This exercise can bring up powerful emotions, so remember to look after yourself. Remember to be ready to enjoy a self-care activity, straight afterwards.

Now that you have finished working through this chapter, review the writing you have done and complete the following sentence stem:

- The main insight I gained from this chapter...

Take a moment, now, to acknowledge all your hard work.

Finally, if you would like a reminder, at any point, that you already have the resources you need at your disposal, you may wish to refer to Grace's poem, below.

Buried

I cannot think or breathe
I feel stuck, I'm buried deep inside the earth
I am suffocating deep beneath the ground
What is happening to me?
Covered up, screaming and shouting but no one can hear me
I am gasping for air, it is tight in here
Dark, dark place, eyes covered like shutters on a plane window
I am so scared, what am I to do?
I need to be on the surface not knocking around in this confined, coffin-like space
I need to find myself in areas that only I can access, before life passes
Slowly, slowly I am moving, breathing
Slowly, slowly but surely
I can smell the grass, the flowers, the air
I do realise that I have a pair of feet, a pair of hands, a pair of eyes and ears
I can feel. Touch, see – and see me
My eyes are open to my misgivings and now I am living
Truly living, not dying inside of myself

Grace Roach

To sum up...

- Uncover the payoff of negative behaviours, so that you can release yourself from them.

- It is important to become familiar with – and understand – your own process of letting go.

- Writing an unsent letter can be a cathartic and rewarding experience.

In the next chapter, we will focus on the way in which your perception of a situation can prevent you from moving forward.

Chapter 7

Changing perceptions

We don't see things as they are. We see them as we are.
Anaïs Nin

Glass half full or half empty

We all see the world though different lenses – the lenses of our experiences, successes and shortcomings. The way we view a situation often determines how we deal with it. If our perception is skewed towards the negative, for example, then this might cause us to respond in an unnecessarily defensive or hostile way. Crucially, however, we each have the power to change our perspective.

We will look at this in more detail, shortly. First, let's explore the concept of seeing the world "as we are". In the exercise that follows, I invite you to write, in response to the quotation at the start of this chapter, from author and short story writer, Anaïs Nin. In my view, her words accurately sum up the nature of perception.

Read the Anaïs Nin quotation aloud, paying attention to any emotions or thoughts that come to mind. Imagine what you would say to someone else, about your reactions to the quote.

- Write instinctively and continuously for five minutes. Let the pen be your guide.

- Read over what you have written and then complete the following sentence stem:

I notice or I am surprised to find…

In her poem, *Why Writing?* - at the end of Chapter 1 - Victoria Field mentions that writing, 'changes the past and creates the future'. There is an important element at play there: perception. We cannot change events from the past. If we have been abused, bullied, betrayed or mistreated, in any way, the facts remain the same. What we *can* change, however, is whether we dwell on the past and give it the power to control us. As individuals, we perceive and respond to the events of our life based on lessons we have learnt - and their reinforcement. Once these patterns are established, it can be a huge task to change our default settings. We have the power, nonetheless, to decide whether events will affect our confidence and ability to bounce back. We can change the way we choose to perceive both the past and present - and, in turn, change our response.

It has been said that there is no reality, only our perception of what is in front of us. The filters through which we view the world create our reality. In other words, whatever happens to us, in our lives, the crucial thing is how we interpret these events. The meaning we give them will determine our outlook and response.

As an example, I would like to mention an issue that often arises in my counselling work, with couples. Perhaps unsurprisingly, couples frequently end up discussing domestic chores with me. The issue of "taking out the rubbish bin" is a common topic. It may seem trivial, but the meaning attached to the simple act of taking a full bin outside is significant. It can reveal a great deal about the way couples communicate and relate to one another.

Let's look at the example of a couple named Cheryl and John. A typical argument between them unfolds like this:

> *It is Thursday night. Cheryl has asked John to place the rubbish bin just outside the front door, ready for collection the next day. By 10pm, however, John has not managed to do so. When Cheryl notices this, the meaning she attaches to his omission is deeply personal. As far as she is concerned, John's lack of action means that he does not care about her. In fact, he cannot really love her, because if he did then he would have remembered to take the bin outside - this is Cheryl's belief. John is, after all, quite aware of all the other things that Cheryl has to do, such as making the children's packed lunches for school, getting the older children ready for bed and feeding their nine-month-old baby. For John, however, moving the bin is just another task on his equally long list of things-to-do. He has picked up their six-year-old from guitar practice, has an important deadline to complete for work and has also agreed to help a friend with moving to a new house. As sometimes happens with a full list, he has simply forgotten about the*

bin! He cannot understand why Cheryl has become so upset. The way he sees it,
he can still take the bin outside a bit later; it is not a big deal.

In this scenario, the facts of the event remain the same: the bin has not been taken outside by 10pm. Cheryl, however, perceives "taking out the bin" as an act of love. John, meanwhile, perceives the same activity as a chore that he could do later. Prior to counselling, Cheryl has never communicated the importance that she has assigned to the bin-emptying chore, at a personal level – and neither has John.

Communicating our needs involves some level of vulnerability. It is essential that we express our feelings and ask for what we want in our relationships. We cannot expect others to read our minds and know what we need.

What is your interpretation of Cheryl and John's situation? Who do you feel empathy for? Is Cheryl in the right, or is John? Is it possible that they are both right about what has happened? We know that the facts remain the same, but the people's two perceptions are different.

How you choose to perceive an event is down to you. Perhaps your inability to see another perspective is getting in the way of creating the future you desire. How do you generally interpret events which have taken place in your life? Reflect on this, in your writing, as you complete the exercise that follows.

This exercise will involve giving your life a title – as if it were a book. The title you choose will give clues as to what you have experienced and how you interpret events. If, for example, Cheryl completed this exercise based on her recent issues with taking out the bin, she might call her book, "Unloved and Uncherished". John, meanwhile, might call his own book, "Just Another Chore".

- If you were to give your life story a book title, what would it be?

- Why did you choose this particular title?

- If you increased your resilience by a few notches – and your book became a number one bestseller – what would the title be then?

- List the chapters of your book in chronological order.

- Create an acknowledgments page, ensuring that you thank and acknowledge all the people who have helped you, in some way, during your life.

- Look over your list. Who, if anyone, seems to be missing? Do you need to make any further amendments? If so, write them down now.

- Read over this whole section of your writing and complete the following sentence stem:

When I read this, I realise…

B r e a t h i n g   S p a c e

Remember that therapeutic writing can leave you feeling drained, so do remember to schedule in regular breaks. It may be useful for you to take a break now, before you move on to the next section.

Altering your perspective

There are times when it is important to alter or shift your perspective, to enable you to move on from a negative experience. In a moment you will be invited to see a difficult situation, through the eyes of a trusted adviser. This new perspective could help you deal more effectively with an issue you are facing.

When my 'Writing for Self-Discovery' group tried this exercise, Liam, a bubbly, 36-year-old, checkout assistant – and self-confessed party animal – decided to write in the voice of his wise grandmother. She helped him to deal with the resentment he felt towards his father, for leaving the family suddenly, when he was aged twelve. Here is the piece that Liam wrote:

> Liam,
>
> I want to get straight to the point. What I have seen is a relationship that, throughout the years, has broken down. I see you both hurting. Your father is a much older man now. When he left his wife – your mother – and the family, he was about the age you are now. He genuinely didn't appreciate the hustle and bustle of London; he longed for home and a more peaceful life in the coun-tryside. He didn't want to spend the rest of his life feeling miserable. So, he thought, with the wisdom he had at the time – and a pretty determined spirit – that he could start again and build a new life for his family, back in Ireland. He didn't know that things would turn out the way they did. He was a proud man, and felt he couldn't embarrass himself and admit that things didn't work out. So, rather than quitting while he was ahead, he sank further and further into

the abyss. It appeared that he didn't care about you, but, honestly, he did. In fact, you were the apple of his eye! He is an older man now and, deep down, he is fully aware of the mistakes he made; but, as a proud man, he could never acknowledge the pain and suffering he caused.

Liam, my advice to you is, try and let it go… This happened a long time ago; release him and send kind, loving thoughts his way. When you pray, ask God to remove all the hurt that you carry around with you. A scripture I recite, that helps me cope when things have not worked out as I have wanted is Romans 8:28, KJV: 'And we know that all things work together for good to them that love God, to them who are the called according to *his* purpose'.

Liam, you know you are a wonderful person, and loved by many. You have a great future ahead of you. Watching you hurt like this tears me apart.

"Nan"

After writing this piece, Liam was surprised by his own words and felt that the energy towards his father had shifted. He felt he was able to see things from his father's perspective, with more clarity – and to understand his father's impact, both on himself and other people. This kick-started a process of forgiving his father, for walking out on him years earlier – and it helped Liam to begin letting go of the pain.

Now it is your turn to seek out a new perspective, by writing from another's point of view:

- Identify a difficulty or conflict you are currently facing. It could relate to a situation where there is some friction or tension, someone you would like to forgive, or an experience you would like to let go of. Describe the situation using a maximum of **five words**.

- Now, identify someone whom you believe is wise – for example, a guardian angel, God, a grandparent, your resourceful self or intuitive self. Write down the name of this wise being.

- Write as if you were this wise being and describe the situation as you see it. Say what you think should happen next.

- Read over what you have just written. Identify a word, phrase or line that you feel connected to, or that is calling for your attention. Circle, underline or highlight the word, phrase or line.

- Using your chosen word, phrase or line as a prompt, write for three minutes.

Breathing Space

Use **3, 2, 1**: Look around you. Notice three things you can see and two things you can hear. Now take one, deep, cleansing breath.

Old perceptions

It can be extremely difficult to let go of the perceptions, thoughts and feelings you have experienced in the past. Perhaps you went through a difficult break-up or were let down by a loved one. It may be hard to imagine that your feelings towards the other person will ever change. However, letting go of our old perceptions and embracing a new image of our world is crucial for building resilience and moving on.

Take a look at Emma's poem, below, and reflect on the process she went through, to change her perception of her situation and herself. She saw 'a glimpse' of the person she wanted to be and this motivated her to leave a psychologically abusive relationship.

It is worth noting here that if you are experiencing domestic abuse*, you are not alone. It is vital you tell someone and seek support from a specialist domestic abuse organisation. This will help you to think about your own situation and explore the best options for you. Leaving an abusive relationship is a process, and a hugely complex and deeply personal decision that needs to be considered carefully. Whilst it can be an incredibly stressful time, there is support available, to enable the process to be managed safely.

Leaving was Emma's decision, before she accessed support; it might not be yours.

Let Go

1
Innocent and naïve
Eager to please and to be pleased
You used this against me
Used my kindness and heart
Until I was nothing

2
Scared to confront you
Scared to confront myself
It was a dark secret kept from the outside world
From the ones who loved me
Who really loved me
3
I tried so many times to escape
But my heart didn't let me
You didn't let me
Others tried to show me the reality
But I had lost sense of reality
4
After time and time again failed attempts of escape
I went away
Away on my own
I exorcised my fears
The fog that blurred my vision was slowly lifted
I could almost see fully
5
So sick of you, sick of the me I was with you
Sick to the point I could not stand it
I'd seen a glimpse of the person I wanted to be!
I refused to let go this time
Except I could finally let go, of you.

Emma
Inspired by Portia Nelson's poem, **Autobiography in Five Short Chapters**

You may not have experienced Emma's situation, but her motivation and need for change might resonate. In the writing exercise that follows, you will have the opportunity to choose between three sentence stems that have been inspired by Emma's poem.

Read the poem, *Let Go* a few times, slowly; read it aloud to feel the words in your mouth and get a sense of its rhythm and beats. Pay attention to any emotions or memories it stimulates in you and imagine what you would say to someone else about your reactions to the poem. When you are ready, complete one of the sentence stems that follows. Write for fifteen minutes.

- I see a glimpse of the person I want to be…

- The fog that blurs my vision is slowly lifting…

- I refuse…

Now, complete the following exercise:

- Read over the piece that you have just written. Identify some words or phrases that resonate with you, or are calling for your attention. Circle, highlight or underline them. Choose one word or phrase and then use this as a prompt. Write for three minutes.

- Read over what you have just written and complete the following sentence stem:

Now that I have read what I have written, I realise…

How did you get on with this exercise? What realisations have come to the fore?

Wendy, a Year 9 student from Richmond Park Academy, shares her own realisations, in the poem that follows.

Only You Can Realise

As I began to love myself
I realised that loving myself is much easier than I thought

As I began to love myself
I realised that everyone has a theory behind their madness

As I began to love myself
I realised that people come and go for a reason

As I began to love myself
I realised that everything happens for a perfectly good reason

As I began to love myself
I realised that love and hate can make you a better person.

Wendy
Year 9 Student

B r e a t h i n g   S p a c e

Pause to appreciate your hard work. Allow yourself to take a deep breath, have a yawn and stretch your limbs.

Crying serves an important purpose

Did you gain fresh insights from the last exercise? Beginning to 'realise' and change your perception of a situation may involve releasing strong emotions, ensuring that the fog can clear. This might mean giving yourself permission to cry.

In the story that follows, read about Robert – and how his father's attitude towards crying shaped his own actions, in later life.

Robert, a 53-year-old senior bank manager, had not cried for years. This was in spite of the fact that his partner, Hannah, had recently experienced her second miscarriage. He began counselling because he did not know how to support his partner through this tragedy.

Robert was also struggling to cope with long hours at work to manage a demanding workload. Not allowing himself to release his emotions meant that pent-up feelings of anger, frustration and sadness were bubbling under the surface, frequently. As a result, Robert often felt anxious and unable to relax.

In counselling sessions, Robert consciously – and sometimes unconsciously – held back a natural response to cry. He blocked a release path for his emotions. His counsellor spent time in their sessions exploring this pattern and also considered its roots. Robert was an only child and grew up with a loving and nurturing mother, but an overly critical father. He recalled the time he came home from school, beaming with pride after achieving a "B+" grade for a school project. His mother was out that afternoon, so he ran to tell his father, instead, who was doing the gardening at the time. His father showed little interest and dismissed Robert's efforts. He insisted Robert only share his efforts if he received an "A"! Robert was disheartened and began crying. Rather than comforting him, his father made fun of him – and then continued to mow the lawn. Robert learned, quickly, that it was not wise to show his feelings, especially his tears, as it often ended up in him being ridiculed and on the end of put-downs.

We will come back to Robert in a moment, but, for now, we are going to look at beliefs associated with shedding tears. You will have a chance to reflect on your own beliefs and experiences in the next exercise.

Challenging your beliefs

When working with my counselling clients and therapeutic writing groups, I am often amazed at the intensity of the response that arises from the subject of tears. Lively discussions occur and I hear expressions such as, 'I can't cry in front of others', 'Tears are a sign of weakness', 'I have to be strong' and 'Crying is for wimps'. Those sentences reflect just a few of the strong beliefs that people hold, frequently.

Such beliefs often stem from our earlier experiences, especially childhood – just as in Robert's situation. As mentioned earlier, in Chapter 3, beliefs are thoughts and ideas that we hold to be true and accurate. In the normal scheme of things, we do not question them. You do, however, have a good opportunity to question some of those beliefs, now. So, let's go ahead and try that. Work through the following questions, noting down your answers as you go.

- What messages, spoken or unspoken, did you hear in your childhood that helped to form your beliefs about crying?

- Which people in your life gave you these beliefs?

- Which of these beliefs now prevent you from crying in your adult life?

Giving yourself permission to cry

It can be difficult to let go of beliefs from childhood. In your own family, you might have been ignored, humiliated, or made to feel stupid if you cried. Some people may have heard gender-specific messages such as, 'Boys and men are not supposed to cry'. This was something Robert's father drummed into him. Read the second part of his story, here:

> *Robert learned from his father that crying was considered to be undignified and childish. He frequently heard phrases such as, 'Tears don't solve anything'. Sometimes, when crying, he would be reprimanded with a threat of punishment, expressed as, 'If you don't stop crying, I will give you something to cry for.'*
>
> *In his counselling sessions, when Robert initially experienced a deep emotion, he fought back his tears. He hated feeling vulnerable. It took him back to all those difficult experiences with his father! Eventually, however, he was able to give himself permission to cry. This allowed him to explore his underlying emotions and speak honestly about his feelings. In addition, linking his feelings to events helped him understand himself better.*
>
> *Robert did not want to become like his father and was extremely fearful that he would be the same type of parent. After having spoken so openly in counselling, he found he was becoming more open in all of his relationships. With his partner Hannah, he shared the heartache of losing their two unborn children and not knowing what to do. He also began to talk about his difficulties at work. Needless to say, his relationship with Hannah improved and they became more supportive of one another.*

Robert discovered that, when he gave himself the permission to cry, he was able to connect with his own emotions more effectively and open up to the people in his life. These might be areas you would like to work on, too. It is always worth remembering that crying is a natural response and can be an important part of letting go and moving on.

The following exercise will help you take a step towards giving yourself permission to cry.

- Consider the answer, or belief, that you wrote down in the last exercise. Write it down again, now. Counter any negative belief, this time, with some new, positive beliefs to help release your tears. Write the new beliefs down.

- Complete the sentence stem:

If I give myself permission to cry…

Can you recall the last time you cried? If you have not had a good cry recently, in response to a deep emotion, do schedule in some time for your tears. Do not force them, but when an emotion arises, try not to suppress any tears. What can you do if the tears do not come? Recently, I was fortunate enough to attend the London Literature Festival at the Southbank Centre and heard activist and poet Nikki Giovanni "In Conversation". She mentioned that 'Learning to cry is a skill'. It is worth remembering these words, when you experience strong feelings. Be kind to yourself and give it time.

When the tears do flow, finally, allow them to fall graciously, as in Emma's poem, below, in which she reminds us that tears are our friends, here to help.

Tears

A teardrop falls graciously and
Slowly down the side of my nose
It holds the little pain I feel in it, I don't wipe it away!
Just let it fall, drip. It's just
like a smile that sits graciously
on my face stretching from
ear to ear showing the joy
I'm feeling in that moment in
time.
Tears and smiles should
go hand in hand, they are not
enemies, they are friends, your
friends, there to help, they are all
one, they are emotions, they are you.

Emma Afia
*Inspired by Alison Gawne's poem, **A Teardrop**.*

The next time you give yourself permission to cry, ask yourself the following questions - and note down your responses as soon as you can:

- What feelings or emotions do my tears represent? Write for seven minutes.

- Where in my body are these emotions or feelings located?

- If my feelings were a body of water, such as a stream, river, lake or the sea, what would they be and why?

- How will I allow my feelings to be expressed?

Changing your perception about tears can take time. The new ideas will need to be integrated into your existing belief system.

In her poem, overleaf, Bukola writes in the third person (using "she" instead of "I"), to articulate her own process of crying and moving on.

She was strong in the wind

When she felt like the person inside needed to escape.
It was a terribly painful process, but she was courageous and determined.
Although gaining a new job propelled her into the daunting, blinding spotlight, she continued to develop and progress.
The pain of breaking through her comfort zone led to a morning ritual of tears and affirmations.
The tears finally dried up, four months later.
The pain started to ease.
Six months later, the pain morphed into mere discomfort.
She was able to recognise she had achieved her goal.
She was now a big step closer to unveiling the 'real' her to the world.

Bukola Charles
inspired by Kenji Miyazawa's poem, **Strong in the Rain**

Now that you have finished working through this chapter, review the writing you have done and complete the following sentence stem:

- The main insight I gained from this chapter…

Take a moment, now, to acknowledge all your hard work.

Finally, if you would like a reminder, at any, point about how waterfalls know the languages of tears, you may wish to refer to Bethany's poem, below.

Tasting Waterfalls

Your waterfall could be the thunderous pourings
     of Niagara or the softer whisperings
         of Pistyll Rhaeadr
   My waterfall plays childhood stories
     of the Butterfly House at Roundhay –
      tropical colours fluttering beyond
          reach of ice-lolly sticky fingers

          Waterfall small –
        as wide as two best friends
        facing the sun together.
     Not very tall
       no more than ten feet
         enough to crick my four year old
      neck

Crystal sheets of nature's hair falling
too fast for your eyes to catch
longer than any scream –
Water falls solid and liquid –
   like love
      like laughter
       like memories
         like the bonds between families

The veins of the world
   kissing the bones of the earth

Waterfalls know the languages of tears
the bows of grief and sorrow
        the dances of ecstasy and joy

Close your eyes
        Listen
        Unfurl your fingers
            caress her flowing hair

            follow the flow of your own waterfall –

Bethany Rivers
Reproduced by permission from Bethany Rivers.

To sum up...

- Perception involves us seeing things through our own lenses.

- Looking at a situation through another's eyes can help us change our own perspective.

- Early messages about crying can prevent us from releasing our emotions.

In the next chapter, we will focus on the way in which being assertive can help you to protect your precious time and energy, and ultimately increase your resilience levels.

Chapter 8

Prioritising self-care

Caring for myself is not self-indulgence, it is self-preservation, and that is an act of political warfare.
Audre Lorde

Self-care in modern times

In our society, being human often involves a poor work-life balance, punishing schedules and the compulsion to be constantly on the go. We lead such busy lives that "switching off" can be seen as a luxury, rather than a necessity. It is no wonder that we become stressed and anxious. Our bodies were not designed for this type of pressure, nor for the demands we are placing on them. It is time to pause and ensure that looking after ourselves is our number one priority.

There are many reasons this can be difficult, of course. These range from the misconception that self-care is selfish, through to the challenges involved in saying "no", to other people. We will explore these in more detail in this chapter. Let us start by focusing on assertiveness and exploring how it can help us to look after ourselves.

The value of asserting yourself

Being assertive is an essential component of self-care and self-preservation. According to the *Cambridge English Dictionary*, 'Someone who is assertive behaves confidently and is not frightened to say what they want or believe'. Assertiveness is not to be confused with rudeness, nor aggressive behaviour. None of the following is assertive behaviour: being angry, being violent, taking advantage of others, or ignoring another person's feelings. I have seen countless people believe, wholeheartedly, that they were engaging in assertive behaviour, when, in fact, they were being rude or aggressive.

Being assertive should, ideally, be a win-win situation, in which both parties' views are respected and valued. You may not always get what you want, but you have an opportunity to express yourself authentically.

At the other end of the spectrum, passive behaviour describes what happens when people take no action at all to influence a situation; instead, they let others take control. This behaviour means that they do not stand up for themselves.

A variation includes people who remain passive while, at the same time, holding onto anger. They are known as "passive-aggressive". Grumpiness and sullenness are often the only visible signs of their anger. It is sometimes difficult to recognise this type of behaviour; it is, nonetheless, immensely impactful – and very unpleasant when you are on the receiving end!

We all behave rudely and aggressively once in a while, or may sulk or seem grumpy. The goal, however, is to aim for *assertive* behaviour.

How assertive are you?

Try this quiz, from *The Self-Esteem Coach: 10 Days to a Confident New You* (Watkins, 2012), reproduced by permission from Lynda Field.

Assertiveness quiz

Check out your behaviour status by answering the following questions:

At home

1. Does your family ever take you for granted?

2. Do you do more than your fair share of the domestic work?

3. Would you like more time just for yourself?

4. Is it hard to say "no" to family members?

5. Do you ever buy clothes and hide them from your partner?

At work

6. Does your job interest you?

7. Are your colleagues appreciative and supportive?

8. Do you always work late when asked, even if you don't want to?

9. Are you able to express your opinions if you disagree with your boss?

10. Would you like to work somewhere else?

Being yourself

11. Do you often compare yourself to others?

12. You have achieved success and someone compliments you. Are you able to accept this gift gracefully or do you brush it off?

13. Do you often feel intimidated when you meet new people?

14. Would you like to be more relaxed with others?

15. Do you ever find yourself apologising for your behaviour?

In a relationship

16. Does your partner make you feel good about yourself?

17. If "yes", how do they do this? If "no", how do they do this?

18. Do you have any shared goals?

19. Are you waiting for your partner to change?

20. Do you still fancy your partner? If "no", why are you together?

Out in the world

21. You reserve a table at a restaurant and find it is at the back, near the door to the kitchen. Do you ask to be moved?

22. A pair of shoes split a month after you bought them. Would you take them back? Would you feel anxious if you did?

23. You think that your child is being bullied at school. Would you investigate further? Would you ever make a complaint?

24. You are on a diet, and friends try to persuade you to eat fish and chips with them. What do you do?

25. Your partner is over the alcohol intake limit but insists on driving. Do you allow it, call a taxi or insist that you drive?

Consider the implications of your answers. Notice the situations where you find it easy to stand up for yourself and those where you do not. When are you most susceptible to letting others "walk all over you"?

Now that you have completed the quiz and answered Lynda Field's questions, write down the answers to the following questions.

- In what areas of your life do you need to be more assertive?

- What do you need to change? Write for fifteen minutes.

Saying "no"

You may have discovered from your answers to the quiz that saying "no" – sometimes or most of the time – is a challenge for you. However, author Amit Kalantri tells us that:

'Real freedom is saying "no" without giving a reason.'

What does this quote mean to you? Let's go through an exercise that involves writing in response to it. Read the words out loud, slowly, and pay particular attention to any emotions or thoughts that come to you.

- Write in response to the quote. Write instinctively, without thinking, for six minutes.

- Read over what you have just written and complete the following sentence stem:

I remember…

The disease to please

In my experience, saying "no" is one of the key issues for people who struggle with confidence and maintaining resilience. I have observed people, over the years, who have the "disease to please" – the people-pleasing syndrome highlighted in Harriet B. Braiker's similarly-named book, *The Disease to Please* (McGraw-Hill, 2001). Later in this chapter, we will explore the story of Sarah, who suffered from the disease to please. Deep down, she yearned for everyone to like her. Is this an issue for you?

If you are not careful, you can spend all your time focusing on other people's needs, while neglecting your own. Of course, we want to help others where we can – in fact, we can feel good when we are providing assistance to others. It is essential, however, that this is balanced with valuing yourself and honoring your time and priorities.

Why do you avoid saying "no"?

"No" can be an extremely difficult word to say to another person. There may be many reasons you want to avoid turning someone else down, even if it will cause you considerable inconvenience. Here are some of the reasons given by participants at my workshops who find it difficult, saying "no":

- 'I don't wish to disappoint someone'

- 'I don't want to hurt the other person's feelings'

- 'I believe the other person will not like me'

- 'I feel the other person will take offence and I will lose the relationship or friendship'

- 'I don't want the other person to get angry'

- 'I don't want a confrontation; it's easier to say "yes"'

- 'If someone asked, they must need it more than I do'

- 'The other person's needs are more important than mine'

- 'I don't want to be judged'.

Do any of these reasons sound familiar? Saying "no" helps you set and maintain healthy boundaries in your relationships. This means other people understand what is – and is not – acceptable to you. Let us have a go at an exercise that will help you explore this topic further.

- What is the main reason you avoid saying "no"?

- Read over what you have written and complete the following sentence stem:

When I read this, I notice, or am surprised to find…

Breathing Space

Use **3, 2, 1**: Look around you. Notice three things you can see and two things you can smell. Go and smell those two things now, then take one, deep, cleansing breath.

What happens when we refuse to say "no"

In the previous section, we looked at the reasons we find it hard to say "no". It is worth considering here that, when we refuse to say "no" to another person, we are actually saying "no" to ourselves!

By continually giving to someone else, when we are in need – whether we are giving our time, energy or resources – we are denying ourselves. We are saying to ourselves that we are not as important as that other person. We also open ourselves up to being taken for granted.

Let us go through an exercise, now, to establish the full impact of saying "yes" to others and "no" to ourselves.

Think of a time when you said "yes" to a request, even though you would have preferred to say "no". Write down the answers to the following questions:

- What was the emotional cost of saying "yes"?

- What was the cost to your time of saying "yes"?

- What was the cost to your energy of saying "yes"?

- What were you depriving yourself of?

The art of saying "no"

I am not suggesting you start saying "no" to every request – consider each request carefully. It is important, nevertheless, to include "no" in your vocabulary. It is worth noting that you are not responsible for other people's feelings and reactions. The important thing here is to be sensitive to a request, while still getting your message across assertively – using a pleasant and warm tone in your voice. Keep practising until it feels right. Bear in mind that you can always tell the other person that you need time to think about their request and will inform them of your answer later. Do not fall into the trap of saying, "I might". Be authentic and tell the truth, but do not make excuses or justify your reasons. A simple, "I prefer not to" or "I am sorry, I can't help on this occasion" will do. If you are feeling brave and want to experience real freedom, do as Amit Kalantri – mentioned earlier in this chapter – suggests and say "no" without giving a reason!

The idea of saying "no" may sound daunting, so, to give you some encouragement, let us focus our attention on the positives. In Chapter 4, we explored the power of using an acrostic to focus thoughts positively, around a particular issue or concept. As you may recall, an acrostic is where we use the letters of a word or phrase, written vertically down the page, to create relevant sentences horizontally.

Have a look at Nicky's acrostic, below, and use this as a source of inspiration as you prepare to complete your own "Saying No" acrostic.

Staying silent
Amongst all the
Yes's allows for
Internal
Nourishment and
Growth
…all that external pressure is
Now
Over

…And i
Now
Own this

NO

Nicky Smit

Now it is your turn to affirm the positives of saying "no", by writing an acrostic.

- Write the words "Saying No" vertically down the page of your notebook or journal. For each letter, write something that will help you when you want to turn down a request and protect your time and energy. You can write one word or several.

S...
A ...
Y...
I...
N...
G...

N...
O...

Making time for yourself

Saying "no" is essentially putting yourself first and practising self-care. Taking the time to look after yourself is vital if you want to increase your resilience levels. As is often said, 'You cannot pour from an empty cup'.

Read the story that follows and discover how Sarah learned to put herself first.

Sarah was married with two children, aged three and nine. She was working full time for a local solicitor when she attended a six-week group, called 'Writing for Self-Discovery'.

On the first evening, Sarah explained to the group her firm had recently won a large contract. When her manager asked if she could take on more work, Sarah said yes, readily. She also offered assistance to her colleagues and would often stay late to help out.

Sarah suffered from the disease to please. She always came across as extremely helpful, yet became anxious and resentful as she tried to please everyone. She rarely said "no", to her detriment. Deep down, one of her goals was to encourage everyone to like her.

Sarah revealed how guilty she felt in leaving the children with a childminder, while she worked late. Her husband, Tom, travelled a 60-mile round trip for work each day, which meant he would never get home in time to take on the childcare.

*When Sarah was introduced to the poem, **Marks**, by Linda Pastan, the words reso-nated with her. She told the group how she felt dissatisfied with her marriage and* *thought she was falling out of love with Tom. She became irritated when he talked about how well he was doing in his job – and there were frequent arguments. As Sarah talked more about her home situation, she admitted she was so stretched by her work, taking care of the children, her domestic commitments and putting herself last, that she often felt very low. She couldn't remember the last time she went out with friends or attended her favourite yoga class.*

It finally reached the stage where Sarah resented both her work and her commitments at home. She couldn't understand, initially, why she felt this way. She had always wanted to be a mum and a career woman. One evening at her self-discovery group, however, she was invited to write out her weekly schedule. When she shared it with everyone else, it became clear, very quickly, that she needed to say "no" more often.

As a first step, Sarah decided to discuss the situation with her husband. It was important that she explained how difficult things were for her, instead of assuming that he knew. Sarah and Tom considered their financial position carefully and agreed that they could make cutbacks. If Sarah worked part-time, they would still be able to manage.

With more time and energy on her hands, Sarah started going to yoga classes again. She routinely took time out for herself without feeling guilty. Needless to say, the resentment disappeared and her relationship with Tom improved! Facing the problem head on also helped the couple to recognise that they needed more time together, without the children. They began setting aside regular "date nights", at home and, every so often would go out for dinner or to watch a movie – just like in the old days. By being honest with herself and Tom, Sarah was able to make space in her life for the nurturing activities that she so needed.

Sarah discovered that her mood and outlook improved, vastly, once she started focusing on her own needs. As mentioned at the start of this chapter, one reason we may struggle to put ourselves first, is the belief that, if we practice self-care, we are somehow being selfish. This idea can lock us into self-sacrificing behaviours.

The next time you do something for yourself – for example, deciding not to go out with friends because you have had a tough week and are exhausted – ask yourself, are you being selfish, or are you exercising self-care?

I would, in fact, like to suggest going one step further. Schedule an activity in your diary or planner that is solely for you – and commit to doing it on a regular basis. You will soon reap the rewards of valuing yourself more, by increasing your self-worth – and, in turn, adding to your resilience bank.

The concept of putting yourself first is explored in the poem below, by Natasha Lynne Vogdes. She talks about getting 'off other people's subways', in other words, moving out of their way and focusing on you. Read the poem; afterwards, you can write in response to it and explore the way you may become "snowbound" in your own private space.

Snowbound

There is a time to stop traveling . . .
to get off other people's subways
to halt airplanes from landing in your life.

A time to refuel yourself.
A time to be snowbound
within your own private space
where the only number you dial
is your own.

Natasha Lynne Vogdes
From **Social Work** *Vol. 25. Issue 1, January 1980 © Natasha Lynne Vogdes.*
Reprinted by permission of Oxford University Press.

Writing in response to a poem
Read the poem, *Snowbound*, slowly, several times. Read it aloud to feel the words in your mouth, and get a sense of its rhythm and beats. Pay attention to any emotions or memories it stimulates in you. Allow the images to come alive.

Next, write in response to the following questions:

- Where do you find yourself in this poem? Is there a particular line or phrase you can connect with or call you own? Use this line or phrase as a prompt. Write for six minutes.

- Whose subway do you need to get off?

- What airplanes have recently landed in your life?

- How can you halt airplanes from landing in your life?

Choose one of the sentence stems that follows. Write for fifteen minutes:

- Now is the time to refuel…

- A time to stop…

- My own private space…

Breathing Space

Place your feet firmly on the ground, drop your shoulders back and focus on your breath. Observe how each intake of air goes into your nostrils and out again, through your nose or mouth. Do not force or alter the breath; just pay attention to it.

Going deeper

Now that you have taken a moment to relax, we will explore the writing you completed in the previous exercise.

- Identify some key words or phrases from your writing; you may feel a strong connection with them or sense them calling for your attention.

- Circle, highlight or underline them. Use these words or phrases as a prompt to start a new piece of writing. Write for three minutes.

- Read over what you have written. Complete the following sentence stem:

Now that I have read what I have written, I notice/feel…

Your self-care list

How do you feel about the idea of making space for yourself every day? Alicia, a participant at one of my workshops, responded to the prompt, 'Today', by creating the piece of writing that follows. With her cancer now in remission, she talks about putting the effort in to love and look after herself.

Today I feel good, inspired, hopeful, excited just to be here, in a therapeutic writing group, as I know how good it's made me feel before.

I feel safe and enthusiastic; there is a chance for me to get a bit better and start to feel well again.

I can only do this if I put the effort in to love and look after myself.

Alicia

Now, consider the ways that *you* can put the effort in to love yourself and practise self-care.

- Start a list of twenty ways you can look after yourself.

- Put the list aside for a couple of days and then add to it again.

Nurture yourself until it becomes a habit

Ultimately, "putting the effort in" means making self-care a priority – and a daily ritual. It can seem challenging at first. My advice is to start small; you may soon come to realise that small changes in your routine can make a huge difference.

In the story that follows, Matthew discovers the value of focusing on self-care activities within his life.

> *Matthew was a social worker who had a large case load, working in the "early intervention" team. He lived in a shared house with people he did not know very well, and he certainly did not make self-care a priority.*
>
> *Matthew's working day started by responding to emails on his bus journey to the office. He was usually the first person to arrive – and one of the last to leave. He had lunch at his desk every day and only took breaks when absolutely necessary. Matthew worried about not seeing much sunlight in the winter, as he seldom left the office before 6pm.*

This routine eventually led to him feeling frustrated and anxious. He had little time for his friends or family, and struggled to get a good night's sleep – since he was often up late, worrying about his work.

Matthew knew he was heading towards burnout*. He felt out of control. After seeing his GP, he was signed off for three weeks. Matthew would have to make some drastic changes, to avoid burnout in the future.

He began life coaching, to help him to figure out what he wanted from life and how to manage stress. He started setting goals and working towards them. He also shared his work situation with his flat mates and began socialising again. It felt good! Matthew attended boxercise classes with his friends and included group meditation in his weekly routine. He was beginning to nurture himself.

Over time, this nurturing became a habit and he felt much more confident. He felt ready for whatever challenges came his way, whether they were work-related or otherwise.

Matthew was able to include a wide range of self-care activities in his life. To help you decide where to focus your own energy, consider the self-care guidance that follows.

Get active

Does your list, from the previous exercise, of twenty ways you can look after yourself include getting active? The benefits of being active are widely known. Physical exercise can help to reduce the risk of heart disease, stroke, type 2 diabetes and other major illnesses. We also know that exercise has considerable benefits for our emotional and mental health.

You may have an injury or disability that prevents you from undertaking specific activities. If this is the case, consider what other forms of exercise you can try. My suggestion is to start small but, before you start at all, consult your GP about the best course of action.

Allow joy into your life

Self-care is not limited to physical exercise. It is also important to have fun and do things you enjoy. When was the last time you carried out an activity you love – for example, visiting an art gallery, taking a trip to the theatre or going to a comedy club and laughing uncontrollably? When did you last use your creative skills and attended an online, writing group or art class? You may be amazed at how quickly your mood and energy changes, once you start reigniting your passions and doing the things you love on a regular basis. This also applies to trying out new activities.

Aim for natural highs

When life becomes challenging, it can be tempting to reach for unhealthy "highs". We can, how-ever, aim for natural highs, instead – healthier ways to elevate a low mood, or just feel really good.

How many of us have occasions of drinking alcohol until we are drunk and then regret it? Or when we have overeaten, even though we were full and trying to lose weight? Perhaps some of us even reach for a drug that has undesirable side effects, knowing that it will cause suffering later on. Matthew, who I mentioned earlier, felt guilty about behaviours like these, but learned there was another way.

> *Matthew often had more than the recommended units of alcohol in a night and also dabbled in recreational drugs. This was a short-term coping strategy that he had previously used – or misused – to reduce stress and anxiety. It gave him a temporary feeling of happiness and peace, but could easily exacerbate his problems and lead to addictive behaviours. He began, instead, setting goals to aim for natural highs.*

Immersing yourself in nature can be one way to achieve a natural boost when feeling low. We can all practise being more mindful, as we enjoy the beauty of nature and being outdoors. According to the *Merriam-Webster Dictionary*, mindfulness is, 'The practice of maintaining a non-judgmental state of heightened or complete awareness of one's thoughts, emotions, or experiences on a moment-to-moment basis.'

A mindfulness practice can help to create a feeling of calm. Next time you see a squirrel in a tree, for example, observe the way it scampers around. Go out for a walk and immerse yourself in the bursts of delightful and distinctive bird song, or the beauty, intricate details and fresh scents of a pink lily. We can achieve a real sense of peace and tranquillity when we are experiencing the joys of nature.

In his poem *The Peace of Wild Things*, featured in *The Selected Poems of Wendell Berry* (Counterpoint, 1998), Berry, the American novelist, poet and environmental activist, talks about being drawn to the natural world when despair grows inside him. By returning to nature, he feels a sense of freedom.

How do you respond to these ideas? Using them as your starting point, I invite you, in the writing activity that follows, to explore the concept of nature as a form of self-care.

- What keeps you awake at night? Write for three minutes.

- What aspect of nature helps you to experience peaceful thoughts?

- Where can you go to experience beauty when you feel low or in despair? Pay particular attention to your senses. Describe what you might see, smell, hear, touch and taste. Include as many sensory details as you can. Write for fifteen minutes.

- Make a commitment to spend some time outside within the next week. Write down a date and time, and say where you will go to experience the beauty of nature.

Nature is a wonderful mood-enhancer. It makes sense to try to get out more, taking advantage of this free, natural resource. If you do so, the chances are you will soon notice benefits to your health and wellbeing. If you cannot get out, for any reason, then perhaps you can bring nature inside by buying a plant, nurturing it and watching it grow and develop.

Now that you have finished working through this chapter, review the writing you have done and complete the following sentence stem:

- The main insight I gained from this chapter…

Take a moment, now, to acknowledge all your hard work.

Finally, if you would like a reminder at any point about the power of nature, you may wish to refer to Gila's poem, below.

A Sun-Kissed Memory

I feel the ocean pushing against me
Each wave knocking me back
The gritty sand burying my feet
The roar of an ocean
Begging to be conquered
And I prevail
I tackle each onslaught defiantly
Jumping each hurdle
Shrieking with each success
Amidst these challenges
All else is forgotten
Thinking back I am transported in time
I feel the sting of the sun and saltwater
On my cheeks

Gila

To sum up...

- Saying "no" is ultimately saying "yes" to yourself and protecting your time, energy and emotions.

- Maintaining self-care is not an act of selfishness.

- It is important to take part in regular exercise, do activities that we love and spend time in nature, appreciating the beauty that is around us.

In the next chapter, we will explore the relationship between fear and courage. We will find out how mirroring other people can add to your resilience bank, and look at what it means to live in the past, present and future.

Chapter 9

Embracing courage

It takes courage to grow up and become who you really are.
E. E. Cummings

Courage is acting in spite of fear

You may have heard the saying that true courage is not the absence of fear, but, rather, acting in spite of fear. What does this mean for you and your journey towards resilience? While completing the exercises in this book, you may well have faced your fears a number of times. It takes courage to change. Moving forward when we are scared, or unsure, is a courageous act.

Some of our fears are, of course, based on our perception of events rather than reality. How often have we allowed our imagination to conjure up the worst thing that could happen and then permitted that *false evidence* to stop us from achieving a dream, or making the right decision? It might be helpful to remember that FEAR can be viewed as an acronym for "False Evidence Appearing Real".

In a moment, we will try writing in response to the poem, *Fear*, by artist, writer and teacher J. Ruth Gendler. This may help you to challenge your fears more effectively. On the next page, read the poem once; we will then go through the writing exercise.

Fear

Fear has a large shadow, but he himself is quite
small. He has a vivid imagination. He composes
horror music in the middle of the night. He is not
very social, and he keeps to himself at political
meetings. His past is a mystery. He warned us not to
talk to each other about him, adding that there is
nowhere any of us could go where he wouldn't hear
us. We were quiet. When we began to talk to each
other, he changed. His manners started to seem
pompous, and his snarling voice sounded rehearsed.

Two dragons guard Fear's mansion. One is ceramic
and Chinese. The other is real. If you make it past the
dragons and speak to him close up, it is amazing to
see how fragile he is. He will try to tell you stories.
Be aware. He is a master of disguises and illusions.
Fear almost convinced me that he was a puppet-
maker and I was a marionette.

Speak out boldly, look him in the eye, startle him.
Don't give up. Win his respect, and he will never
bother you with small matters.

J. Ruth Gendler
*From **The Book of Qualities**, by J. Ruth Gendler. Copyright © 1988 J. Ruth Gendler. Published
by Harper Collins. Used by permission of the author.*

Writing in response to a poem

Now is your chance to respond to Gendler's poem. Read the poem again, slowly and if possible – out loud, to feel the words in your mouth and get a sense of their rhythms and cadences.
Pay attention to any emotions or memories the poem stirs in you. Imagine telling someone else
about your reaction to the poem. What would you say?

- What is your emotional response to this poem?

- Is there a line you could call your own? Use this line as a prompt. Write for six minutes.

- What stories has fear tried to tell you during your life?

- Take a phrase, word or line from the poem that evokes the strongest response in you and use it as a prompt for a piece of writing. Write for ten minutes.

- Read over what you have written. Now, underline, circle or highlight anything that feels insightful or meaningful for you. Use this as your prompt. Write for ten minutes.

Breathing Space

Stop and relax. Feel your feet on the ground and follow your breath, in and out, a few times. Take a moment for yourself.

Delving deeper

In her poem, J. Ruth Gendler says that we need to speak out boldly, look fear straight in the eye and 'startle him'. How can we achieve this? Let's delve a little deeper with the help of a "cluster" – also known as a mind map or spider diagram.

- Turn to a blank page in your notebook or journal. In the middle of the page, write the word "Fear". Draw a circle around it and then begin to free-associate. Spin thoughts off from other thoughts, recording them on your page using single words or short phrases. Be spontaneous; do not stop to think about or edit what you are writing. Keep the pen moving until you fill the page – or have exhausted all your ideas.

- You have just created a cluster. Spend a few minutes reflecting on your cluster. Read the words aloud; then choose one word or short phrase from the cluster and write whatever comes to mind - for ten minutes.

Did you write anything that surprised you or which you found interesting? When we write things down, we open ourselves up and allow our unconscious voices opportunities to speak spontaneously and authentically. You may have experienced this with your cluster or with previous writing tasks. Our writing helps us to peel back the layers and discover what lies beneath.

We are about to carry out an exercise that will help you to look fear straight in the eye and peel back the layers. The activity may appear to involve some repetition. Even though you might be keen to get on with your personal development, this particular process will mean taking things more slowly. Whilst you might find this challenging, initially, there is value in staying the course.

- Read over your last writing exercise. Identify the words or phrases that resonate with you or are calling for your attention. Circle, highlight or underline them. Then choose one word or phrase and use this as your prompt. Write for three minutes.

- Read over your piece of writing. Again, identify the words or phrases that resonate with you or are calling for attention. Circle, highlight or underline them. Use these as a prompt to start a second piece of writing. Write again for three minutes.

- Read over your second piece of writing. Once more, identify the words or phrases that resonate with you or are calling for attention. Circle, highlight or underline them. Use these as a prompt to start a third piece of writing. Write for a further three minutes.

- Reflect on your third piece of writing and complete this sentence stem:

I am aware…

Breathing Space

Use **3, 2, 1**: Look around you. Notice three things you can see and two things you can hear. Now take one deep, cleansing breath.

Living from a place of authenticity

How did you find the last exercise? Did you uncover what lies beneath your fears? Or did your writing take you to somewhere else, unexpectedly?

If you are courageous enough to be your authentic self, in spite of your fears, you will then be in a strong position to realise your full potential and honour your highest values.

Jamie, mentioned previously in Chapter 4, was determined to live out his values despite - what others said. Read more about his experiences in the section that follows.

Jamie wanted to realise his full potential in the music industry. This was something he valued highly. He sometimes found it a challenge, however, to be his authentic self. Being himself didn't seem to fit with other people's views of who he was, or should be.

His brother, a doctor, would often joke about Jamie's choice of career and ask him, 'Why don't you get a proper job – one with more security?' But Jamie loved the music business. He enjoyed seeing his artists get signed, release a debut album and delight fans at a gig. Determined to live out his values, Jamie refused to worry about what other people might think. He did not change himself to meet the expectations of others, nor fit in with their beliefs, as he knew it would be a never-ending journey.

Jamie found his brother's attitude to be a source of pressure. Perhaps you first felt the weight of other people's expectations within your family of origin. Where we come from often has a bearing on whether we feel able to be courageous in later life – and be true to who we are.

Let's consider your own origins, now, by writing in response to a poem by Imelda Maguire, an Irish poet born in Kildare and raised and educated in Limerick. She is a practising counsellor who facilitates creative and personal development groups in Ireland. The poem, on the next page entitled *Origins*, is featured in Maguire's book, **Shout If You Want Me to Sing** (Summer Place Press, 2004).

Origins

I come from a bog-cotton,
hawk-cry, flat, plain place;
from a father who was
a motherless boy.
I come from a factory-chimney,
mouth-of-the-river city;
from a line of strong, proud
women, good with their hands;
from a mother who was
eldest of eight,
working at twelve,
keeping house for families
where children older than she
were cosseted and sent to school.

I come from someplace
between the cold that called
for greatcoats piled on the bed
and the white-hot heat of
a Saturday night range;
somewhere between the piety
of nightly rosary and the radical
words of my father, berating the clergy
who persecuted the last few
Limerick Jews.

I come from times that were changing
and carry a residue of times
that never will.

Imelda Maguire
Reproduced with permission from Imelda Maguire.

Writing in response to a poem

Now is your chance to respond to Maguire's poem. Read the poem again, slowly and – if possible – out loud, to feel the words in your mouth and get a sense of their rhythms and beats. Pay attention to any emotions or memories the poem stirs in you. Imagine that you are telling a close friend or confidante about your reaction to the poem. What would you say?

- What is your emotional response to this poem?

- Where do you come from?

- Is there a line you could call your own?

- What qualities are apparent from the women in your family?

- What radical words of your father do you remember?

- What aspect of your origins hinders your ability to be courageous or resilient?

- I would like to encourage you to create your own "origins" poem. Bear in mind that it is not necessary for poems to rhyme. To start you off, I suggest using the following words in your opening line:

'I come from…'.

- Read over your poem and then complete this sentence stem:

Now I have read what I have written, I notice/feel…

Breathing Space

Stop and relax. Feel your feet on the ground and follow your breath, in and out, a few times. Take a moment for yourself.

Modelling resilience

How did you get on with your "origins" poem? What did you discover? Poems such as these tell the early stories of our unique and precious lives.

In the previous exercise, we looked at your origins and how they may impact your ability to be courageous and resilient. Now, we are going to focus on how you can be more courageous and boost your resilience, by learning from others.

When challenges come our way, we can be sure that someone, somewhere has experienced what we are going through. By tapping into this knowledge and copying – or "modelling" – what a resilient person does, we can evolve our own approaches to life. We can shed past behaviours which no longer serve us. We may decide to finally let go of unhelpful defence mechanisms, such as not fully investing emotionally in relationships. These strategies may have helped us to avoid pain in the past, but now we can learn more effective ways of responding.

So, where do we start? J. Ruth Gendler's poem, *Courage*, talks about courage having roots. Looking back at your own roots, perhaps you notice that you learned about courage from your family or friends.

Donald learned about what it means to have courage and be resilient, through his friend, Shane. Read about their experiences in the story that follows.

Donald's family members were not positive role models and so he needed to look to others in his life for inspiration. His friend, Shane – a retired teacher and, at this time, a taxi driver – had recently lost his partner Joe, to a long-term illness. Donald was impressed by how well his friend was coping with this loss, all things considered. But when Shane was the victim of a robbery, during a night shift, Donald wondered whether it would be "the last straw".

Shane refused to let the attack change his personality, however. He showed no ill-will towards his attacker, who had left him with both physical and emotional injuries. He decided, in fact, that he would return to work within a few weeks. When Donald asked Shane how he was able to deal with everything so well, his friend explained that he was determined to not let what happened in life define who he was. He was more than a grieving partner; he was more than the victim of a robbery.

Shane loved his job. He enjoyed interacting with the public and finding out about their lives. His work was also playing the vital role of keeping him busy, after the loss of his much-loved partner. Shane made sure that he took as many precautions as possible when accepting a taxi fare. He also made an arrangement with his daughter that he would give her a quick call, at the end of every shift, so she could check he was okay.

Donald realised that, for Shane, the only way to get through this difficult period of his life was to make adjustments and carry on. This took courage and Donald admired him for it.

Shane proved to be a positive role model for Donald. All of us can learn valuable lessons about resilience by being around friends, colleagues or family members who are courageous and have well-developed resilience skills.

Identify the people in your life who are resilient and have bounced back from adverse situations. Look for, or create an opportunity to strike up a conversation - where possible - so you can ask them what they did and how they used courage to see them through. Perhaps you can add some of their skills to your own resilience toolkit.

Let's explore this further, now, through a writing exercise.

- Identify someone who you would describe as being resilient. This could be someone you know, personally, or someone famous whom you admire from a distance. It does not matter whether this person is alive or dead; they could, even be a character from a television programme. Try not to spend too much time thinking about it. Use your instincts and write down a name…

- Jot down an example of an adverse experience during which the person, or character, showed resilience. Aim for two or three words, only.

- Write down what they did, specifically, to overcome the adversity.

- List the skills or tools they used. If you are not sure, try to imagine the skills that they would have used.

- What skills or tools could you add to your resilience toolkit?

List them.

- Now, create a piece of writing, entitled, "**Embracing Courage**". This could take the form of a poem, speech, or any other form of writing that you feel comfortable with.

Living in the present moment

We have, so far, explored the ways in which we can challenge fears. We have begun to look at our origins and have considered how to gain resilience by learning from others. Over the sections that follow, we will be looking at how to change the focus of our "thinking" time, in order to build resilience even further.

In my experience, many people spend a lot of their thinking time focussed on one of two time zones: the past or the future. Learning from past experiences or planning for future events can be extremely worthwhile. Spending too much time thinking about the past or the future can, however, be counterproductive – particularly if we are focusing on negatives. It can mean we miss out on valuable and precious moments in the present, which prevents us from appreciating who we are – and what we have – in the here and now.

Where do you usually focus your attention? Do you find it difficult to be present? I invite you to explore this further, in the exercise that follows.

On which time zone do you focus most of your thinking time? Write it down.

a. Past

b. Present

c. Future

- What benefits are there to spending most of your thinking time in that zone?

- What disadvantages are there to spending most of your thinking time in that zone?

- What have you learned from this exercise that can help you to be more present, and able to live in the moment?

Coming back to the present

I offered the following exercise as a warm-up, during a workshop that I facilitated to celebrate International Women's Day (8th March). The day is dedicated to advocating women's rights and recognising the achievements of women who have fought to overcome adversity.

For the warm-up, I invited participants to write in response to the word, "Here". It is a valuable exercise in mindfulness, since it encourages the writer to reflect actively on the present moment. The following piece was produced by Caitlin, one of the workshop participants:

Here I am. Inside a circle of potential friends, celebrating International Women's Day. Here I've chosen to be and become something a little different than yesterday. A cup of lemon-ginger tea; I read on the tube that it's good for circulation - right now. Here. I drink it.

There is much power in the immediacy of a solution that just comes into being. So, it's great to be here - in a setting I've never experienced before - in Camden, a place I don't frequent often. It's amazing how my thoughts were all over the train this morning, splattered around the walls, windows, seats. Big, wild, untamed thoughts about big themes; I was truly on a roller coaster of cognitive process.

Then, to mark the day and focus my attention, I chose to read Oriah Mountain Dreamer's poem, *The Dance*, and I realised how most of my life is one, big, flowing dance. One of delegating energy, allowing flow and blocking it, moving with it and finding my footing in how I relate to it, in each and every "here" and "now", ultimately becoming a channel for the energy that creates universes. So, right now, I could be that channel, if I choose. Although sometimes I'm tired of thinking about what I could be... Life is really about the experiencing of experience.

Caitlin Bracken

I invite you, now, to try the same exercise and see where your writing takes you.

- Complete the sentence stem that follows and write whatever comes to mind. Do not stop to edit or think about what you are writing. Keep the pen moving. Write for six minutes on the sentence stem:

Here…

Capturing positive moments

In her piece of writing, Caitlin mentions that life is really about, '…the experiencing of the experience'. With that in mind, let us relive a positive experience, by capturing a moment from your life. Read through both parts of the exercise before you get started, so that you can gain the full experience.

- Make yourself comfortable. Focus your attention on the here and now, feeling your feet on the ground and the chair supporting your body. Follow your breath. Observe it moving in and out for a few moments. Close your eyes or lower your gaze. Reflect on the past six months – or a timeline which feels appropriate for you. Now, allow a positive memory to arise in your thoughts. Notice which particular moment from that memory is calling for your attention. Allow any images to come alive. Keep focusing on that one, pleasant moment and spend some time absorbing it. If any unpleasant memories start to occur, open your eyes and do not continue further to focus on them. You can go, instead, straight to the writing part of the exercise and describe the initial pleasant memory. If, however, you are struggling, currently, to find a positive experience, overall, you may want to take a break and come back to this exercise later.

- For those who can continue, now, when you are ready, open your eyes and begin to describe the memory on paper, using the first person and present tense, (that is, "I am…"). Pay particular attention to your five senses of sight, smell, sound, touch and taste. Include as many sensory details as you can.

You can return to this exercise whenever you need to lift your spirits. Writing about positive experiences releases endorphins that help make us feel good. Doing this type of writing on a regular basis also allows us to recreate pleasurable moments and keep them alive in our minds.

Looking beyond the present

Being resilient may mean looking beyond your present situation. If the moment you are in feels uncomfortable or unpleasant, then you will need a way to reassure yourself and pull yourself through. Having a motivational phrase – or several phrases – that you can repeat during difficult times is extremely valuable.

In the story that follows, Jada experimented with many ways to numb the pain, after being abused as a child. She eventually found a way through.

When Jada was 12-years-old her uncle came to stay with the family for a while, having recently separated from his wife. Jada was delighted. She loved her uncle, who would often bring a huge bag of sweets for her and her younger sister. He took a special interest in Jada, helping her with schoolwork and playing guitar with her. They would jam together for what seemed like hours on end!

One day, Jada's parents went to visit her older sister, who was struggling to cope at university. That day, her uncle sexually abused Jada. The abuse continued over the next two years. Her uncle threatened to harm her and her younger sister if she told anyone.

Jada began falling behind at school and became withdrawn. Sometimes she was overly anxious or angry – she couldn't control her mood swings. She stopped hanging out with her school friends and spent a lot of time on her own.

Jada wanted to tell someone, but didn't feel that she could. 'Who would believe me?' she thought – and, instead, began experimenting with drugs as she tried to numb the pain.

Jada also became involved in a string of abusive relationships. She didn't plan to become a mother, but children soon came along. Her boyfriends also introduced her to hard drugs, which led her to self-medicate and ultimately, to move into a life of crime. She began stealing to feed her habit.

Things started to turn around, unexpectedly, when Jada ended up with a short jail sentence. The judge was lenient in his sentencing. For the first time in her life, she felt that someone was showing her compassion.

Jada hated being in prison. She missed her family and children terribly, but she also felt a sense of solidarity with the other women. Some of them spoke about being abused. Until this point, Jada had thought she was the only one.

Jada wrongly believed she was a bad person and that the abuse was her fault. It took time for her to eventually disclose her abuse to a drugs worker, when she was released from prison. Jada believed that prison saved her. It was the point she turned her life around and made the decision to heal. This became the start of Jada's healing journey. Although she had not finished school with any qualifications, she had always enjoyed journaling, so, when her drugs worker suggested a therapeutic writing group, she agreed to give it a go. She was adamant that she did not want her scars to define her.

After completing a detox programme, Jada, then aged 31, attended a poetry therapy group for survivors of sexual violence. The group used poems as a springboard for discussions and writing. Through this, she explored various ways to heal from her experiences. Jada attended regularly. Even when it was tough, she stayed with the process. After reading **The Summer Day***, a poem by American poet Mary Oliver – who won both the National Book Award and Pulitzer Prize – Jada answered the question Mary had posed in the last line of the poem:* **'Tell me, what is it you plan to do with your one wild and precious life?'** *Jada began to believe that her own life was precious. She wanted to help other women – in any way she could – and began volunteering at a local drugs charity.*

Jada suffered a traumatic start to her life. It took courage to begin the healing process. If you are – or have been – in a similar situation, then I encourage you to seek support. Find an organisation that specialises in providing services for survivors of sexual violence, when *you* are ready. Healing from your experience can help you to enjoy the beauty life can offer.

Breathing Space

Stop and relax for a moment. Feel your feet on the ground and the chair supporting your body. Follow your breath; observe it moving in and out. Do this a couple of times and then stretch.

Precious, a survivor of sexual abuse and a workshop participant, responded to the following writing prompt: **"This too shall pass…"**. Here is the poem she wrote.

This Too Shall Pass

This too shall pass
like when my teeth were hurting
I went to the dentist to get it fixed.

This too shall pass
like the day I
lost everything.
This too shall pass
like the day my
world came crashing in on top of
me which left me stuck for years.

This too shall pass
when anger grows
inside me when I had to face my
past with no answers to hear.

This too shall pass
like when the
day all except one of my children got taken away
and my child I had left said she
hated me.

This too shall pass
the feeling of dislike
in myself because I know it's only for today.

This too shall pass
when I crave
for that drag and I feel I
really need it.
At the times I feel like life is just too much, a voice in my head says,
'THIS TOO SHALL PASS'.

Precious

The phrase "This too shall pass" has been a source of inspiration within Middle Eastern folklore for centuries. It is a wonderful reminder that no matter how challenging things are right now, these difficult feelings and memories - or their intensity, at least - will not last. They shall - and, indeed, do - pass.

You may not have experienced sexual violence, but "This too shall pass" is a useful phrase when any situation is overwhelming.

Breathing Space

Stop and relax. Feel your feet on the ground and follow your breath, in and out, a few times. Take a moment for yourself.

When you are ready, take this opportunity to create your own poem, by following the instructions in the next exercise.

- Use the writing frame* from Precious's poem, *This too shall pass*, to create a new poem:

This too shall pass…
    I lost …
    My world…
    Inside me …
    When I …
    Feeling …
    At the time…
    A voice…
….This too shall pass.

- When you have finished, give your poem a title.

Breathing Space

Therapeutic writing can leave you feeling drained, so do remember to schedule in regular breaks. It may be useful for you to take another little break, now, before you move on to the next section.

Coping with future difficulties

We have looked at the concept of living in the present moment and explored using a motivational phrase to help you get through difficult times. Next, we will discover how focusing on the future, in a positive way, can help you manage challenging situations.

In their book, *How to Deal with Stress* (Kogan Page, 2007), Stephen Palmer and Cary Cooper offer a useful stress management tool that involves visualising yourself coping with a challenging situation – and which I have adapted slightly. Perhaps you know, in advance, that you will be having a difficult conversation with your boss. Or you might be about to embark on a new role as the main carer for a loved one. Maybe you need to discuss changes in the family, with your children. Try this exercise when you know, ahead, that difficulties are around the corner.

Coping imagery

Step 1: Think of a situation in the future that you are worried about.

Step 2: Note down in your journal, or notebook, specific aspects of the circumstance that you are stressed about. Highlight, circle or underline the ones that instinctively feel most stressful.

Step 3: Brainstorm and jot down all ideas to cope with these difficulties.

Step 4: Read the visualisation text through – at least twice – before getting started. Perhaps you could record the visualisation using the "voice" function on your smartphone. When you come to perform the visualisation, you might find it helpful to keep your eyes closed, throughout. If you feel uncomfortable, however, or find the visualisation is not working for you, open your eyes.

Visualisation text
Visualise yourself in the situation that you are concerned about. Taking this slowly, imagine yourself coping with each anticipated difficulty as it arises. Pay attention to what you are doing, in particular – and to your senses. What can you hear, as you are coping with each difficulty? Take note of what you can see, as you are dealing with the various difficulties in a positive way. Listen to and/or picture your thoughts, focusing on the nurturing and loving things you are saying to yourself, as you cope with the situation confidently. Pay special attention to the way in which you are naming and managing your emotions, successfully. Visualise the different ways in which you cope with this situation with composure and ease.

Repeat this procedure over the next week. Familiarise yourself with it, so you can make use of it whenever needed – especially when you notice any warning signs in your body that you are becoming stressed about a forthcoming event.

Measuring your progress

We are going to check your current resilience levels. You can use this to help measure your progress from since you started working on enhancing your resilience. Using the checker that follows, you will be able to give yourself a resilience score.

Resilience Levels Checker

Look at the resilience scale, which represents the range of emotions and thoughts from your lowest levels of resilience to your highest. Think about where you would generally place yourself on that scale.

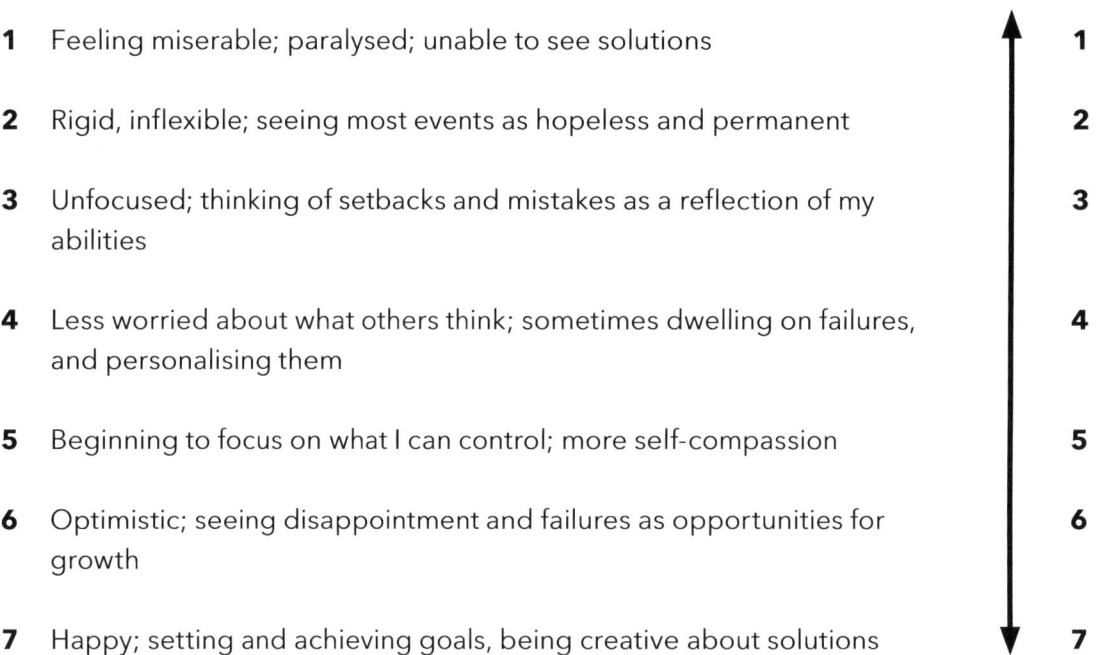

Your resilience at its lowest

1   Feeling miserable; paralysed; unable to see solutions   **1**

2   Rigid, inflexible; seeing most events as hopeless and permanent   **2**

3   Unfocused; thinking of setbacks and mistakes as a reflection of my abilities   **3**

4   Less worried about what others think; sometimes dwelling on failures, and personalising them   **4**

5   Beginning to focus on what I can control; more self-compassion   **5**

6   Optimistic; seeing disappointment and failures as opportunities for growth   **6**

7   Happy; setting and achieving goals, being creative about solutions   **7**

Your resilience at its highest

Where are you on the scale now? Are you at level 4, "Less worried about what others think, sometimes dwelling on failures and personalising them", or level 6, "Optimistic, seeing disappointment and failures as opportunities for growth"?

Take a look in your journal, or notebook, and compare your previous resilience level to this current one. Do you feel a sense of improvement? You may have placed yourself at the same level, but perhaps notice positive changes in your self-talk or behaviours, when you cope with challenging situations.

If you believe that there has not been much improvement, then remember that we all change at our own pace. It is also worth noting that building resilience is not a linear process. Sometimes we will find ourselves going backwards, before entering a period of growth and change.

Perhaps you have, indeed, made positive changes but are unable to see them clearly – yet. The following exercise will go some way towards helping you with this.

New coping mechanisms

The next exercise will use metaphors, to look at the new coping mechanisms you have developed throughout this book – with a view to appreciating the changes you have made and what you have accomplished so far. It can be easy to downplay our progress, particularly when we are accustomed to judging ourselves harshly, or setting unattainable standards.

- Think about both your previous and current coping strategies and consider the differences between them. Next, you will create a two-stanza* poem, using the sentence stems that follow. In the blank spaces, insert two different types of weather that represent your coping strategies. For example,

'I used to be grey clouds, because…' and 'Now I am sunshine, because…'.

Write at least one paragraph for each.

I used to be… [insert weather type], because…

Now I am… [insert weather type], because…

- Compare the two paragraphs and complete the following sentence stem:

I notice…

You can, hopefully, see the difference between where you started and where you are now. Remember to give yourself credit for *all* of your achievements!

Now that you have finished working through this chapter, review the writing you have done and complete the following sentence stem:

- The main insight I gained from this chapter…

Take a moment, now, to acknowledge all your hard work.

Finally, if you would like a reminder at any point of the ingredients that can help you to become more resilient, you may wish to refer to Tee's poem below.

A Recipe for Resilience

2 arms full of forgiveness
3 bucket loads of compassion
1 skip full of hope
4 kilos of patience
5lbs of self-raising love
12 shovel loads of strength
4 handfuls of courage
6 litres of determination
Stir well with a courageous hand.
Bake in the sun for four hours whilst you reward yourself with a glass of champagne.

Tee Falcone

To sum up...

- Courage is acting in the presence of fear.

- Mirroring other people's resilient behaviours can help you develop your own resilience skills.

- Focusing your attention on the present ensures that you do not miss life's precious moments.

In the next chapter, we will concentrate on creating a new and lasting legacy that you can weave into the lives of others.

Chapter 10

Creating a new legacy

What you leave behind is not what is engraved in stone monuments, but what is woven into the lives of others.
Pericles

Leaving an impression

Every day of our lives, each one of us is contributing towards our own legacy. Malika Booker, an award-winning British poet of Guyanese and Grenadian parentage, in her poem, *Burial Ground*, which is featured in the book *Your Family, Your Body*. (Penguin Books, 2017), says, 'There are the marks we leave and those that will be made.'

You are already making and leaving your legacy, mark or imprint, with every idea you have, every choice you make – with every action and inaction. By working on your legacy, you can create considerable change in your own life and leave a heritage that becomes a unique gift to others.

We are going to explore the concept of legacy in more detail, to help you make a conscious decision about the type of legacy you wish to weave into the lives of other people. Let's start by writing in response to the quotation by the ancient, Greek statesman, Pericles, which appears at the beginning of this chapter.

Read that quotation aloud, slowly, paying attention to any emotions or thoughts that come to mind. Imagine what you would say, to someone else, about your reactions to the quote.

- In your journal, or notebook, write the quote down and then complete a free write*. That is, respond to Pericles' words by writing whatever comes to mind. Pour everything out onto your page. Write for ten minutes.

How did you respond to the Pericles quote? Did it help you to consider the legacy you wish to weave into the lives of others?

I was first inspired to further explore the idea of legacy when I attended a National Association for Poetry Therapy conference, in Black Mountain, North Carolina, USA a few years ago. I signed up for the workshop 'Living and Leaving Your Legacy®' by Merle R Saferstein. I was intrigued by the title and knew that the session would help me with my work – particularly with second-generation Holocaust survivors. What I could not know was the way in which the workshop would also apply to my own life and choices. Saferstein discussed the value of legacy work and provided hands-on, practical ways to document memories, life lessons and values. Her workshop helped me to understand more fully that the way we live our lives is the way we leave our legacies.

Saferstein left such an impression on me that, when I returned to the UK, I immediately began to ponder the legacy I wished to leave. What would be my mark? How would I express my highest values, greatest gifts and talents? As I considered this, I realised I was already creating – and leaving – my mark, with every decision, thought or action I took.

The exercise in the following section will help you to explore this concept for yourself.

Fingerprints on a glass

Imagine this scene: you are in the kitchen. Your hands are greasy from cooking or baking a cake and you reach for a glass to have a drink. As you put the glass down, you notice that you have left fingerprints on its surface.

Now picture another scene: you are getting ready to go out and have sprayed on some perfume, or aftershave, to freshen up. You also use some hand cream and immediately reach for a drink, to quench your thirst. The imprint on the glass may still be greasy, but it will be different than in the previous example. Both experiences involve leaving fingerprints; leaving a part of you behind. Whatever you are doing or being in life, you leave an imprint – a personal mark. This is your legacy.

Have you ever considered the effect you are having on individual people - on family, community, or, generally, on your small corner of the world? When hearing about tragedies or adversities, at home and abroad, people sometimes respond by saying, 'I can't change the world', or, 'There isn't much I can do'. I disagree with both these statements! Single individuals *have* changed and shaped our world. You may not leave a legacy that is as far reaching as, say, Martin Luther King, or Emmeline Pankhurst, but *your* fingerprints can grow in certain hearts and spaces - as mentioned in the following poem, by Dee.

Read Dee's poem, now; then answer the questions that follow.

Legacy

I'd like to think that I leave my fingerprints in the most obscure and
unusual places
That invisible part of me is helping me to leave my legacy
everywhere I go
And the beautiful thing is, in some hearts and spaces those fingerprints will grow.

Dee Morrison

- In what 'obscure and unusual places' will your fingerprints be left? Write your thoughts down.

- Who would you like to see benefit from the mark that you leave on this world? Write for three minutes.

- What could you do, now, to make this happen?

A roll of 'loving tape'

In her poem, *Woman*, at the end of Chapter 3, Nicky Smit suggests there is so much wrong with this world, that she keeps 'a roll of loving tape' to mend her heart, every time it breaks. A piece of advice I would like to offer is for everyone to wind 'a roll of loving tape' around them, whenever their heart breaks.

I have also enjoyed being the 'roll of loving tape' for many other people, throughout my life – especially in my career. I consider this to be my legacy.

Later in this chapter, you will have the chance to explore what you consider to be your legacy. Firstly, let us look at the legacies that have been left to you, by your family of origin. Families come in all shapes and sizes. You may have come from a single parent family, two parent family or a blended family. You may, alternatively, have been in care, or grown up in a foster home – or, indeed, several foster homes – or been adopted into a family that was, or was not, related to your birth parents.

Whatever type of family you experienced, though, it is essential to recognise and challenge anything negative in the family legacy that could hinder your ability to cope with your struggles.

The legacies you inherited

Matryoshka dolls, commonly known as "Russian dolls", form a set of wooden nesting dolls stacked inside one another. Each doll splits in half and opens to reveal another, smaller doll.

You are already carrying the legacies inherited from your own family. Legacies have been passed on to you, from previous generations – and they live on inside you, similar to the idea expressed in the design of the Russian Matryoshka dolls.

Nikki Giovanni, mentioned, previously, in Chapter 7, is an African-American, Tennessee-born professor, poet and GRAMMY Award finalist in the 2003 Best Spoken Word Album category for *The Nikki Giovanni Poetry Collection*. Through her work, she is leaving her own, remarkable legacy for future generations to learn from. Her legacy can be summed up as one of courage and resilience. In overcoming cancer and other challenges, she has gone on to accomplish staggering achievements. Giovanni is the author of numerous children books and poetry collections. She was the first recipient of the "Rosa Parks Woman of Courage Award". Several magazines have also named her, "Woman of the Year", including: *Essence*, *Mademoiselle*, *Ebony* and *Ladies' Home Journal*.

Giovanni's poem, 'Legacies', which is featured in the book *Selected Poems of Nikki Giovanni 1968-1995* (William Morrow, 1996), opens with a grandmother calling a little girl in from the playground, to teach her how to make rolls. We learn so much from our grandparents, parents, significant carers and – in some cases – extended family. Through our family members, we learn about our culture, values, religious and spiritual beliefs, and the wider world. These are developed and shaped in our early years.

We inherit characteristics and traits from our family members – and witness and learn both positive and negative behaviours from them. This may have been evidenced in your own *'Origins'* poem, in the previous chapter. What we absorb in our formative years has an impact on our later life experiences, including the types of partners, friendships and relationships we choose. It also impacts the way we relate to others, particularly if we do not challenge some of our beliefs. You are probably aware that you are still enacting some of the behaviours you learned from your family, care home or carers, while others may have been adapted, or even discarded.

Jamaican-born professor and poet, Lorna Goodison, has earned several awards for her writing and poetry. She explores the concept of inherited traits in her poem, *I Am Becoming My Mother*, featured in *Being Human*, edited by Neil Astley (Bloodaxe Books, 2011). Do you ever hear yourself saying things that your mother, father, foster parent or significant carer used to say? Perhaps you recognise, as you get older, that you are becoming similar to them in many ways. Does that mean you will pass on the same legacy? Some people who have experienced abusive, difficult or unhappy childhoods do not want to be like their parents or carers and spend their lives trying extremely hard to be different. We saw an example of this with Robert, in Chapter 7, who did not want to repeat the specific traits and destructive patterns of his father. The good news is, you can change the legacy you have inherited and make the choice to pass on positive behaviours to your children, or the people around you.

In the first instance, let us see what legacies have been passed on to you, and identify how similar or dissimilar you are from your parents or significant carers. Finding similarities and differences can be very revealing. We will use metaphors for this exercise, as they offer a useful way to tackle what may otherwise seem a challenging task.

Read Stuart's piece, below, for inspiration, before you go on to complete the exercise that follows.

My mother was a flimsy tent which was always in fear of the weather.
But I am a prison that is safe from the storms but also hidden from the sunlight.

Stuart

In this exercise, you will be filling in the blanks. It may seem daunting at first. Swapping people for objects could feel like a challenge. I hope I can encourage you to try this exercise, nevertheless. You may be surprised by what your writing reveals!

- Complete this writing frame, using the instructions that follow:

My [first blank space] was a [second blank space]

But I am a [third blank space]

1. **In the first blank space,** insert the title of your significant carer when you were a child, for example, mother, father, aunt, foster mother, care home worker, grandmother and so on. If you did not grow up with a particular family member, but would still like to complete the exercise using that person, then try to imagine what they may have been like.

2. **In the second blank space,** insert a place of residence to act as a metaphor for that person, for example: a hotel, cottage, castle, caravan – and so on. Add some details to explain why you have made this choice.

3. **In the third blank space,** insert a place of residence to act as a metaphor for yourself, for example: a hotel, cottage, castle, caravan, house, apartment – and so on. Add some details to help explain why you have made this choice.

- Read over what you have written and then complete this sentence stem:

Now I have read what I have written, I notice/feel…

Once you have completed this exercise, for one parent or significant carer, I suggest you repeat it with other family members, or carers, who were influential in your childhood. This will help you identify your inherited legacies. From there, you will be able to gauge how similar to - or dissimilar from - your current legacy those given to you by others were.

Breathing Space

Stop and relax. Feel your feet on the ground and follow your breath, in and out, a few times. Take a moment for yourself.

Leaving a positive legacy

How did you get on with the previous exercise? What did your writing reveal? We are about to move on from focusing on the legacies you have inherited, to choosing the legacy you wish to leave. Lara, a workshop participant, writes, in her piece, below, about the way she wishes to be remembered.

Legacy

It is enough for those who love me to know and remember me. I don't need to be famous, or known for some great achievement, to have had a meaningful and worthwhile existence.

What I want most is to have people in my life who love me and feel that I matter and make a positive difference to their lives, by being in it. I want them to think that my "dash" is of value and worth.

Lara

Inspired by Linda Ellis's poem, **The Dash**

Lara is referring, in her poem, to the dash or line usually engraved on a headstone, between the date you were born and the date of your death. Lara clearly states that she wants her "dash", or, in other words, her life, to be of value and worth.

- How will your life be of value and worth? What will your dash represent? Write for fifteen minutes.

I invite you, now, to explore your legacy using the concept of a eulogy. This is a speech or piece of writing, read out at a funeral, which celebrates the life of the person who has died. For some people, discussing a legacy – and imagining what people might say about them when they are gone – might feel morbid. This can be particularly true in the case of recent bereavement. If you are someone who has been bereaved, recently, it may be better to come back to this section later, when you will feel more able. However, in another case, you may feel that it is fine to continue.

For those who are ready now, let us find out how exploring your eulogy can help to focus your mind on what matters in your life.

Occasionally, when I have attended the funeral of someone close to me, the eulogy has mentioned that person's passion for a hobby, for an incredible skill they had, or an interesting job they held when they were young. Yet I did not know that detail about the person. I have re-flected on, and regretted the missed opportunities for, the discussions we could have enjoyed – if only I had known.

What are the key things you want the world to know about you? Take a moment to explore this, in the exercise that follows.

- What would you like to be included in your eulogy? How do you want to be remembered? What would you say must be mentioned without question? Jot down a few thoughts that immediately come to mind.

- Now respond to the following question: What must not be left out of your eulogy? Write for ten minutes.

Writing your eulogy

You managed, hopefully, to find at least one thing that must not be left out of your eulogy. Let us now begin to put together your full eulogy. Writing your own eulogy may seem a little daunting. Completing this exercise will, however, help you to identify your priorities and clarify your values. Identifying and honouring your values is at the heart of creating and living your legacy. As you may recall, we looked at the importance of values in Chapter 3, but you may like to refresh your memory on this, briefly, at this point.

Before you begin to write your full eulogy, think about the important aspects of your life. What matters most to you? What lessons have you learned that you would like to pass on? Consider what you have contributed to your family, and/or community – and how you have touched vari-ous individuals, no matter how light or heavy the touch was.

For added inspiration, you might like to refer back to the writing you completed for Chapter 3, where you identified your core values – and in Chapter 5, where you explored your dreams and aspirations.

Now is your chance to bring all of these ideas together. In order to write your eulogy, you may find it helpful to use the sentence stems below, as prompts. Do remember to write about yourself in the third person and past tense, for example, "He was…", "She was…", or, "They were…".

- She/he/they was/were born…

- She/he/they enjoyed…

- She/he/they gave… to this world.

- She/he/they overcame…

- She/he/they will be remembered by…

Breathing Space

When you have finished, take a deep breath, yawn and/or stretch. Remember that therapeutic writing can leave you feeling exhausted, so do remember to schedule in regular breaks.

Living your legacy
How did it feel to write your eulogy? Perhaps you were able to clarify the aspects of your life that are particularly important to you. Let's build on this momentum by translating it into action.

- Describe one action that you can take in the near future to help ensure that you are remembered for something that is important to you. Write for ten minutes.

- Now turn to Chapter 5, "Awakening the Dream", and, using the step-by-step guide, "Action Planning for Success" (from the middle section of that Chapter), apply the information that you have just detailed, during the first part of this exercise, above, to set yourself a goal.

Breathing Space

Stop and relax. Feel your feet on the ground and the chair supporting your body. Follow your breath; observe it moving in and out. Do this a couple of times and then stretch.

Creating a ten-point survival guide for your younger self

Now it is time to bring together everything you have learned on your journey through this book. You are about to create a ten-point survival guide.

To prepare for the writing activities ahead, you might like to browse through your journal, or notebook, and recall the exercises and key information that you have found helpful, in terms of building and maintaining your resilience.

We will also consider the words of Margaret Atwood, a multi-award-winning, Canadian writer and author, who has written prize-winning novels, short stories and poetry. Her poem, *Provisions*, featured in the book, *The Animals in That Country,* highlights the pitfalls of going on a journey without being adequately prepared. It poses the question, "What should we have taken with us?" The survival guide that you are about to create will involve you advising your younger self about the provisions you should take on your life's journey. It will be an invaluable resource, created with the help of hindsight, life lessons and the insights you have gained from both this book and your writing.

First, from the list that follows, choose an age from your childhood, adolescence or young adulthood.

Younger self

- Age 5–8

- Age 9–12

- Age 13–18

- Age 19–25

You may find it useful to find a photograph, from the age range you have chosen, to help you remember the experiences you had at that earlier stage in your life. If you cannot find a photograph, can you remember one? Once you have a photograph in mind, complete the exercise that follows.

Spend a few minutes, in silence, looking at – or remembering – the photograph of your younger self. What was the occasion or reason for the photograph? Pay attention to the setting, who was with you, your physical size, your clothes, your hairstyle, your facial expressions – and anything else that stands out. Sit with your emotions for a short while. Then, if necessary, carry out a self-care activity before continuing further.

- Writing for six minutes, now, complete the sentence stem:

When I look at, or remember, my photograph, I see a girl/boy/woman/man/person who…

You are now going to create a list of provisions that you will advise your younger self to bring, on your life's journey. For example, you may wish to bring a book, such as, *Writing Away the Demons*, by Sherry Reiter and Contributors, to remind your younger self about how valuable it is to write down your thoughts and feelings – and be able to read other people's experiences of courage and resilience. You might also wish to bring the quality of self-compassion with you, so that your younger self remembers to offer self-love and nurture, along the way.

- List the provisions for your life journey and write your reasons for taking each one.

Breathing Space

Use **3, 2, 1**: Look around you. Notice three things you can see and two things you can hear. Now, take one deep, cleansing breath.

Creating your survival guide

You have just written down your list of provisions and your rationale for each. What do you think is the most useful provision? Now is your chance to create the ultimate survival guide for yourself. It is the culmination of everything you have learnt about resilience. Take this opportunity to create your unique, ten-point survival guide, to help you survive when adversity comes your way.

- Look back through your journal or notepad and reflect, in your writing, on the discoveries you have made. Using all that you have learnt, since you started doing the exercises in this book, create your ten-point survival guide:

1.

2.

3.

4.

5.

6.

7.

8.

9.

10.

- What do you notice about your survival guide? Did you uncover anything surprising? What - if anything - seems to be missing? Do you need to make any amendments? If so, write them down, now.

- Next, I want to encourage you to take the information from your ten-point survival guide and transform it into a poem. This can be a useful way to remind yourself that you have the resources to endure any situation.

- If you are feeling courageous, take the opportunity to send me a copy of the poem. You can find my contact details at the end of this book. I would be honoured to read your words!

Now that you have finished working through this chapter, review the writing you have done and complete the following sentence stem:

- The main insight I gained from this chapter…

Take a moment, now, to acknowledge all your hard work.

Finally, if you would like a reminder, at any point, about the importance of a legacy and being who *you* want to be, you may wish to refer to Dee's poem, below.

Hair and Back

Legacy, cultural, my heritage
My journey of self-discovery
As a black woman

Family traditions of time with mother
Combing and grooming my hair
The ritual of washing, greasing and plaiting

Coming of age and desires to get
Rid of these kinky black curls
To straighten, to deny
Roots broken down to a curly perm
Or to the iron-flattened look

University, the key that unlocked the door
Time to look in the mirror
And decide who I want to be
Time to be me

The change has come
Back to my roots
Back to my natural tresses
Embracing and loving
And feeling free

Dee Morrison

To sum up...

- Our legacy is the mark we are currently leaving on the world.

- You can start to make changes now, to consciously create a lasting impression of the way you would like to be remembered.

- Maintaining – and regularly referring to – your survival guide, or poem, will help to enhance your resilience.

Thank You

We have almost come to the end of our journey together. I would like to acknowledge your tenacity and sincerely thank you for reading this book.

We all like receiving heartfelt "Thank you" cards; we feel good when someone appreciates our sacrifices, or recognises our efforts. Research on the impact of gratitude letters suggests that we might underestimate just how happy our "thanks" will make the other person. Studies have also shown that expressing gratitude can strengthen our relationships.

Perhaps you are grateful to someone who has stuck by you during difficult times. Or maybe there is someone in your life whom you really appreciate and would like to thank, now. This may relate to something special they did for you, although you might simply want to thank them for being who they are. Whilst the recipient of a "Thank you" letter, or email, can feel happy, so may the writer. It is a two-way street. So, now is your chance – with a last writing activity – to write a letter that will lift your mood, as well as your recipient's mood, helping you to both feel great!

- Write a handwritten, "Thank you" letter; ideally do so to *three* different people in your life, but certainly to at least one person.

- Send your "Thank you" letter(s), doing your bit to encourage the recipient(s) to feel special and appreciated.

As a final thank you, from me, I would like to share with you Roger Robinson's poem, *A Portable Paradise*. It is a reminder that we can find comfort in many different situations, if we carry our own little piece of paradise with us wherever we go.

A Portable Paradise

And if I speak of Paradise,
I am speaking of my grandmother
who told me to carry it always
on my person, concealed, so
no one else would know but me.
That way they can't steal it, she'd say.
And if life puts you under pressure,
trace its ridges in your pocket,
smell its piney scent on your handkerchief,
hum its anthem under your breath.
And if your stresses are sustained and daily,
get yourself to an empty room – be it hotel,
hostel or hovel – find a lamp
and empty your paradise onto a desk:
your white sands, green hills and fresh fish.
Shine the lamp on it like the fresh hope
of morning, and keep staring at it till you sleep.

Roger Robinson
*"A Portable Paradise" from **A Portable Paradise** (Peepal Tree Press, 2019) © Roger Robinson,
reproduced by permission of Peepal Tree Press.*

Glossary

Burnout

Burnout is excessive and prolonged stress that involves a state of emotional, physical and mental exhaustion. It is often associated with work-related stress. It involves feelings of cynicism and negativity towards the source of the stress (for example, a person's job). It also leads to reduced levels of effectiveness.

Catastrophising

This is a common thinking error, where a person focuses on the worst possible outcome of a situation without contemplating the possibility of a positive outcome. For example, you are due to go on holiday and are convinced that the aeroplane you are due to travel in will crash, in spite of all evidence that suggests otherwise.

Coercive behaviour

The definition that was proposed by HM Government, within the 2018 consultation, *Transforming the Response to Domestic Abuse (justice.gov.uk)* 'Coercive behaviour is an act or a pattern of acts of assault, threats, humiliation and intimidation or other abuse that is used to harm, punish, or frighten their victim.'

Cognitive distortions

Cognitive distortions, or thinking errors, are automatic, unhelpful and irrational ways of thinking about something, which do not correspond with the reality of what is actually happening. The thoughts are often negative and can have a huge impact on our stress and anxiety levels, particularly when we do not challenge these thoughts.

Controlling behaviour

According to the definition proposed by HM Government in 2018, as part of the *Transforming the Response to Domestic Abuse (justice.gov.uk)* consultation, 'Controlling behaviour is a range of acts designed to make a person subordinate and/or dependent by isolating them from sources of support, exploiting their resources and capacities for personal gain, depriving them of the means needed for independence, resistance and escape, and regulating their everyday behaviour.'

Domestic abuse

The statutory definition proposed by HM Government in 2018, within the *Transforming the Response to Domestic Abuse (justice.gov.uk)* consultation, describes domestic abuse as: 'Any incident or pattern of incidents of controlling, coercive, threatening behaviour, violence or abuse between those aged 16 or over who are, or have been, intimate partners or family members regardless of gender or sexual orientation. The abuse can encompass, but is not limited to:

- psychological

- physical

- sexual

- economic

- emotional'.

Flow writing, free writing or stream-of-consciousness writing

This technique involves writing down everything that comes into your head, without censorship. You allow your writing to flow, without giving thought to content, structure, punctuation, spelling or grammar. This is often performed within a time limit. It is advisable to not read over your work whilst you are writing, but, instead, to continue placing words on the page until your writing session has come to an end.

Imposter syndrome

Imposter syndrome relates to feelings of self-doubt, and anxiety about being exposed as a "fraud". People with imposter syndrome can believe that any success they have achieved is due to luck, rather than their talents – even when the evidence around them suggests otherwise.

Metaphor

A metaphor is a word or phrase that stands in for something else, in order to explain or enhance that thing. For example, when we say that a situation has gone "pear-shaped", we do not mean that it has actually transformed its shape. We mean that it has gone wrong; it is irregular, like the shape of a pear. We may use metaphors frequently, in daily life, often without realising it. Other common metaphors include, "Between a rock and a hard place", "Barking up the wrong tree" and "The world is your oyster".

Mind reading

In a therapeutic context, this is considered a common "thinking error". It involves assuming that you know what other people's thoughts and intentions are, based on either minimal or zero evidence. For example, let us say that, at lunch time, your colleague, Jim, walks straight past you in the street without acknowledging you. You are convinced that he does so because, either, he does not like you, or you have somehow offended him. In the future you decide to ignore Jim. Sadly, you have let your thinking veer towards the negative, without clarifying things. The more likely reason that Jim walked past you is that he simply did not see you. Perhaps he was caught up in his own thoughts – as many people often are.

Sentence stem

A sentence stem is the beginning of a sentence which you are invited to complete. The stem may be just one word, or several words. The aim is to finish the sentence in your own words, using the stem as your starting point.

Sexual violence

According to Rape Crisis England and Wales, 'Sexual violence is any unwanted sexual act or activity. There are many different kinds, including: rape, sexual abuse (including in childhood), sexual assault, sexual harassment, forced marriage, so-called honour-based violence, female genital mutilation (FGM), trafficking, sexual exploitation (including child sexual exploitation, and others').

Stanza

A stanza is a group of lines used in poetry, where the lines are arranged in a pattern. They are usually grouped by rhythm and/or rhyme. A stanza is similar to, and can be described as, a verse.

Timed writing

With a timed writing activity, you will be informed beforehand of the time allocated to the task. The aim is for you to then complete your writing within the given time limit.

Writing frame

A writing frame uses the framework or skeleton of an existing poem to create a new piece of writing. To begin, you take the first word – or words – from chosen lines of the original poem and write them vertically down the page. You then use this framework as the starting point for your new piece. You might also choose to use the original poem's theme as inspiration for your own piece of writing.

Writing prompts

A writing prompt is any source of inspiration that is intended to spark ideas and help you start writing. A prompt will often focus your mind on a particular concept or topic. Writing prompts come in many forms, including written words, pictures, objects, pieces of music, places and people.

Resources

It is good to have an end to journey towards; but it is the journey that matters, in the end.
Ursula K. Le Guin

You will find some useful resources, here, to offer help and inspiration as you continue on your journey.

Now that you have completed this book, you may wish to consider attending a writing group. Alternatively, now might be the right time to seek the help of a therapist or counsellor, or book a series of life coaching sessions. Any of these options could offer valuable support and would mean that you do not have to journey on alone.

Poems

The following is a list of the published poems mentioned in this book.

Atwood, Margaret. "Provisions." *The Animals in That Country.* Toronto: Oxford University Press, 1968.

Berry, Wendell. "The Peace of Wild Things." *The Selected Poems of Wendell Berry.* Washington, D.C.: Counterpoint, 1998.

Booker, Malika. "Burial Ground." *Your Family, Your Body.* UK: Penguin Books, 2017.

Dickinson, Emily. "Hope Is The Thing With Feathers". *The Poems of Emily Dickinson.* Edited by R. W. Franklin. Harvard University Press, 1999.

Ellis, Linda. "The Dash." *Live Your Dash: Make Every Moment Matter.* New York: Sterling Publishing Company, 2011.

Feaver, Vicki. "Coat." *Close Relatives.* London: Secker & Warburg, 1981.

Field, Victoria. "Why Writing?" *Writing Works: A Resource Handbook for Therapeutic Writing Workshops and Activities,* edited by Gillie Bolton, Victoria Field and Kate Thompson. London: Jessica Kingsley Publishers, 2006.

Gawne, Alison. "A Teardrop." *Words for Wellbeing,* edited by Carol Ross. Penrith: Cumbria Partnership NHS Foundation Trust, 2012.

Gendler, Ruth J. "Courage." *The Book of Qualities. Harper Collins, 1988.*

Gendler, Ruth J. "Fear." *The Book of Qualities. Harper Collins, 1988.*

Goodison, Lorna. "I Am Becoming My Mother" *Being Human,* edited by Neil Astley. Northumberland: Bloodaxe Books, 2011.

Giovanni, Nikki. "Legacies." *Selected Poems of Nikki Giovanni 1968 -1995.* New York: William Morrow, 1996.

Hughes, Langston. "Harlem." *from The Collected Poems of Langston Hughes, 1994, published by Alfred A Knopf Inc, © The Estate of Langston Hughes. Reprinted by permission of David Higham Associates.*

Jennings, Elizabeth. "Into the Hour." *Elizabeth Jennings: New Collected Poems.* Manchester: Carcanet, 2002.

Maguire, Imelda. "Origins." *Shout If You Want Me to Sing.* Ireland: Summer Place Press, 2004.

Miyazawa, Kenji. "Strong in the Rain." *Soul Food: Nourishing Poems for Starved Minds,* edited by Neil Astley and Pamela Robertson. Northumberland: Bloodaxe, 2007.

Nelson, Portia. "Autobiography in Five Short Chapters." *There's a Hole in My Sidewalk: The Romance of Self-Discovery.* New York: Atria/Beyond Words, 1993.

Oliver, Mary. "The Summer Day." *New and Selected Poems.* Boston, MA: Beacon Press, 1992.

Pastan, Linda. "Marks." *The Five Stages of Grief.* New York: W.W. Norton & Co, 1978.

Pastan, Linda. "What We Want." *Carnival Evening: New and Selected Poems 1968-1998*. New York: W.W. Norton & Co, 1998.

Robinson, Roger. "A Portable Paradise." *A Portable Paradise. Leeds: Peepal Tree Press, 2019.*

Rumi, Jelaluddin. "The Guest House." *Rumi: Selected Poems.* Translated by Coleman Barks with John Moyne. London: Penguin Books, 2004.

Oriah Mountain Dreamer. "The Dance." *The Dance.* San Francisco: Harper ONE, 2001.

Stafford, William. "The Way It Is." *The Way It Is: New and Selected Poems.* US: Graywolf Press, 1998.

Vogdes, Natasha Lynne. "Snowbound." *Social Work* 25.1 (1980): 67.

References and inspirational books

Adams, Kathleen. *Journal to the Self: Twenty-Two Paths to Personal Growth.* New York: Warner Books, 1990.

Adams, Kathleen. *Journal Therapy for Calming Anxiety: 366 Prompts to Help Reduce Stress and Create Inner Peace.* New York: Sterling Publishing Company, 2020.

Allen, Summer. *The Science of Gratitude.* California: Greater Good Science Center, 2018.

American Psychological Association (2011). Retrieved from https://www.apa.org/topics/resilience

Bolton, Gillie; Field, Victoria; and Thompson, Kate (Editors). *Writing Works: A Resource Handbook for Therapeutic Writing Workshops and Activities.* London: Jessica Kingsley Publishers, 2006.

Bowman, Ted. *Loss of Dreams: A Special Kind of Grief.* Minnesota: Ted Bowman, 1994.

Braiker, Harriet B. *The Disease to Please: Curing the People-Pleasing Syndrome.* New York: McGraw-Hill, 2001.

Cameron, Julia. *The Artist's Way: A Course in Discovering and Recovering your Creative Self.* London: Pan Books, 1995.

Chavis, Geri Giebel. *Poetry and Story Therapy: The Healing Power of Creative Expression.* London: Jessica Kingsley, 2011.

Covey, Stephen. *The 7 Habits of Highly Effective People: Powerful Habits in Personal Change.* (25th Anniversary Edition). London: Simon & Schuster, 2012.

Craven, Pat. *Living with the Dominator.* London: Freedom Publishing, 2008.

Field, Lynda. *60 Ways to Feel Amazing.* London: Vermilion, 2000.

Field, Lynda. *The Self-Esteem Coach: 10 Days to a Confident New You.* London: Watkins, 2012.

Field, Victoria. *Baggage: A Book of Leavings.* London: Francis Boutle Publishers, 2016.

Fox, John. *Poetic Medicine: The Healing Art of Poem-Making.* New York: Jeremy P. Tarcher/ Putnam, 1997.

Gawain, Shakti. *Creative Visualization – Use the Power of Your Imagination to Create What You Want in Life.* California: Nataraj Publishing, 2002.

Goldberg, Natalie. *Writing Down the Bones: Freeing the Writer Within.* Boulder, Colorado: Shambhala Publications, Inc., 1986.

HM Government (2018). "Transforming the Response to Domestic Abuse: Government Consultation." Retrieved from Ministry of Justice Consultation Hub: https://consult. justice.gov.uk/homeoffice-moj/domestic-abuse-consultation/supporting_documents/ Transforming%20the%20response%20to%20domestic%20abuse.pdf.

Holder, Jackee. *49 Ways to Write Yourself Well: The Science and Wisdom of Writing and Journaling.* Brighton: Step Beach Press, 2013.

Irons, Chris and Beaumont, Elaine. *The Compassionate Mind Workbook: A Step-by-Step Guide to Developing Your Compassionate Self.* London: Robinson, 2017.

Jacobs, Beth. *Writing for Emotional Balance: A Guided Journal to Help You Manage Overwhelming Emotion*. Oakland: New Harbinger Publications, 2004.

Jakes, T D. *Let It Go: Forgive So You Can Be Forgiven*. New York: Atria Paperback, 2012.

The Holy Bible. Authorized King James Version. USA: Zondervan Publishing House.

Kumar, Amit and Epley, Nicholas. "Undervaluing Gratitude: Expressers

Misunderstand the Consequences of Showing Appreciation." *Psychological Science*. 2018 Sep; 29(9):1423-1435.

Maguire, Imelda. *Serendipity*. Limerick: Revival Press, 2015.

Markway, Barbara and Ampel, Celia. *The Self-Confidence Workbook: A Guide to Overcoming Self-Doubt and Improving Self-Esteem*. California: Althea Press, 2018.

McGuinness, Julia. *Writing Our Faith*. London: SPCK Publishing, 2013.

Palmer, Stephen and Cooper, Cary. *How to Deal with Stress*. London: Kogan Page, 2007.

Reiter, Sherry and Contributors. *Writing Away the Demons: Stories of Creative Coping Through Transformational Writing*. Minnesota: North Star Press, 2009.

Robertson, Donald. *Build Your Resilience: How to Survive and Thrive in Any Situation*. London: Hodder Education, 2012.

Robinson, Roger. "Manifesto: Roger Robinson – Success is on you." *The Poetry Review, 107:3, Autumn 2017*. Pennebaker, James. *Opening Up*. New York: The Guilford Press, 1990.

Pennebaker, James. *Writing to Heal: A Guided Journal for Recovering from Trauma and Emotional Upheaval*. Oakland: New Harbinger Publications, 2004.

Pennebaker, James. Opening Up by Writing it Down: How Expressive Writing Improves Health and Eases Emotional Pain. (Third Edition). New York: The Guilford Press, 2016.

Preston, David Lawrence. *365 Steps to Self-Confidence: A Complete Programme for Personal Transformation – In Just a Few Minutes a Day.* Oxford: How To Books, 2001.

Rhimes, Shonda. *Year of Yes: How to Dance It Out, Stand in the Sun and Be Your Own Person.* New York: Simon & Schuster, 2015.

Sanderson, Christiane. *The Warrior Within: A One in Four Handbook to Aid Recovery from Sexual Violence.* London: One in Four, 2010.

Sethi, Anita (13 June 2020). "Roger Robinson: Poets can translate trauma". Retrieved from https://www.theguardian.com/books/2020/jun/13/roger-robinson-poets-can-translate-trauma, The Guardian. [Online]

Sissay, Lemn. *My Name is Why: A Memoir.* Edinburgh: Canongate Books Ltd, 2019.

Thompson, Kate. *Therapeutic Journal Writing: An Introduction for Professionals.* London: Jessica Kingsley Publishers, 2011.

Tutu, Desmond M. and Tutu, Mpho A. *The Book of Forgiving.* New York: Harper Collins, 2014.

Venable Raine, Nancy. *After Silence: Rape & My Journey Back.* London: Virago, 2010.

Weiss, Elaine. *Surviving Domestic Violence: Voices of Women Who Broke Free.* USA: Volcano Press, 2004.

Williams, Mary Beth and Poijula, Soili. *The PTSD Workbook: Simple, Effective Techniques for Overcoming Traumatic Stress Symptoms.* USA: New Harbinger Publications, 2002.

Williams, Nick. *The Work We Were Born to Do: Find the Work You Love; Love the Work You Do.* Kent: Balloon View, 2010.

Useful organisations

Alcoholics Anonymous (AA)
'AA is concerned solely with the personal recovery and continued sobriety of individual alcoholics who turn to the Fellowship for help.'
https://www.alcoholics-anonymous.org.uk/

Alzheimer's Society – United Against Dementia
'From day one of dementia, we'll be right here with you. For support and advice. For campaigning, and one day, for a cure.'
https://www.alzheimers.org.uk/

The Black, African and Asian Therapy Network (BAATN)
'Home of the largest community of Counsellors and Psychotherapists of Black, African, Asian and Caribbean Heritage in the UK.'
https://www.baatn.org.uk/

British Association for Counselling and Psychotherapy
'The British Association for Counselling and Psychotherapy is the professional association for members of the counselling professions in the UK.'
https://www.bacp.co.uk/

Childline
'Childline helps anyone under 19 in the UK with any issue they're going through.
Trained counsellors provide free, confidential telephone support any time, day or night.'
https://www.childline.org.uk/

Clinks
'Clinks supports, promotes and represents the voluntary sector working with people in the criminal justice system and their families. Our vision is of a vibrant, independent and resilient voluntary sector that enables people to transform their lives.'
https://www.clinks.org/

Cruse Bereavement Care
'Cruse Bereavement was founded in 1959 in Richmond upon Thames and is the leading national charity for bereaved people in England, Wales and Northern Ireland.'
https://www.cruse.org.uk/

Lapidus International

'Lapidus International is an expressive arts company that believes in the power of words, both spoken and written, to provide benefits to well-being and professional development. The company supports its members internationally by giving them opportunities to connect, develop and share in the Lapidus community.
https://www.lapidus.org.uk/

Macmillan Cancer Support

'From the moment you're diagnosed, through your treatment and beyond, we're right there with you, offering emotional, physical and financial support.'
https://www.macmillan.org.uk/

Mind

'We provide advice and support to empower anyone experiencing a mental health problem. We campaign to improve services, raise awareness and promote understanding.'
https://www.mind.org.uk/

National Association for Poetry Therapy – USA

'The National Association for Poetry Therapy (NAPT) is a non-profit, interdisciplinary membership organization that supports and enhances the profession of poetry therapy. Its mission is to promote growth and healing through written and spoken language, symbolic expression, and story.'
https://poetrytherapy.org/

National Association of Writers in Education (NAWE)

'NAWE is the one organization supporting the development of creative writing of all genres and in all educational and community settings throughout the UK.'
https://www.nawe.co.uk/

National Domestic Violence Helpline

'The Freephone 24-hour National Domestic Violence Helpline. Tel: 0808 2000 247.'
https://www.nationaldahelpline.org.uk/

Rape Crisis England & Wales

'We exist to improve services and promote the needs and rights of women and girls who have experienced sexual abuse, rape and all forms of sexual violence. We also work towards the

elimination of sexual violence and abuse, raising awareness in the wider community and with government.'
https://rapecrisis.org.uk/

RiseUp
'RiseUp was established in 2015 to empower individuals to better their circumstances, prospects and well-being. RiseUp works with prisons, schools, the long term unemployed and those at risk of offending within the wider community.'
https://www.riseupcic.co.uk/

Samaritans
'Samaritans is a unique charity dedicated to reducing feelings of isolation and disconnection that can lead to suicide.'
https://www.samaritans.org/

Survivors of Bereavement by Suicide
'We exist to meet the needs and break the isolation experienced by those bereaved by suicide.'
https://uksobs.org/

Survivors UK
'We help victims of male sexual abuse as well as their friends and family, no matter when the abuse happened. We are here to support, challenge, build.'
https://www.survivorsuk.org/

The Poetry Society
'Founded in 1909 to promote 'a more general recognition and appreciation of poetry'. With innovative education and commissioning programmes and a packed calendar of performances, readings and competitions, The Poetry Society champions poetry for all ages.'
https://poetrysociety.org.uk/

We Are With You (formerly Addaction, Young Addaction and ThinkAction)
'We Are With You provides free, confidential support to people who have issues with drugs, alcohol or mental health. We work with people on their own goals, whether that's staying safe and healthy, making small changes or stopping an unwanted habit altogether.'
https://www.wearewithyou.org.uk/

Women's Aid

'A grassroots federation working together to provide life-saving services and build a future where domestic violence is not tolerated.'

https://www.womensaid.org.uk/

Young Minds

'We're leading the fight for a future where all young minds are supported and empowered, whatever the challenges. We're here to make sure they get the best possible mental health support and have the resilience to overcome life's difficulties'.

https://youngminds.org.uk/

About the Author

Charmaine Pollard is a counsellor, life coach, college tutor and poetry therapist. She initially trained as a person-centred counsellor, focusing on trauma recovery, where she developed a passion for teaching resilience skills. Charmaine runs regular poetry therapy groups, both online and in the community. She is a former board member of Lapidus International, an expressive arts company that believes in the power of words to enhance mental and physical wellbeing.

Email: charmaine@charmainepollardcounselling.co.uk

https://charmainepollardcounselling.co.uk/

Printed in Great Britain
by Amazon

61997585R00124